Holy Bible Holy Koran

Almighty and All Powerful: Side by Side

David Alalade

ISBN 978-1-4477-6058-0

www.davidalalade.com

Acknowledgements

For mother, who upon discovering my fascination for the written word thought it was an excellent pursuit. Bless her.

Works by the author David Alalade

www.davidalalade.com

Non-Fiction Books

Holy Bible Holy Koran

www.holybible-holykoran.com
www.holybible-holyquran.com
www.holyquran-holybible.com
www.thetwinbooks.com

Short Story Fiction

Sympathy for the Samaritan (pending film adaptation)

Korea Woman

The Great Gambler

Kaarmesin the Murderer

The Marvellous Maurice

The White Bull

Wax Wings

<u>Visit us online</u>

davidalalade.com

holybible-holykoran.com

holybible-holyquran.com

holyquran-holybible.com

thetwinbooks.com

Face book: David Alalade

You Tube: Holy Bible Holy Koran / Book Soundtracks

Listen to the music soundtracks commissioned for the book.

Read the review by the 'U.S. Review of Books'.

With comments & emails from a global readership of fans.

Video reviews from online bloggers, writers, and fans.

A behind the scenes look at upcoming book fairs & events.

And regular updated content on the upcoming sequel:

'Holy Bible Holy Koran 2'

David Alalade, was born to Jide and Margaret Alalade, in Kaduna, Nigeria, in the year 1979. He was raised from age six in London, England, on a diet of healthy living and free-thinking. He began writing short stories at age thirteen having read all the volumes in his family's home library of encyclopaedias and books on world cinema and religion. His interest in ancient books and English literature which was soon discovered, nurtured, and greatly encouraged. David entered his first writing contest at age nineteen to claim first prize and during his mid twenties took an interest in short story fiction writing; resulting in one of his works being selected for a short film adaptation. In the spring of 2009, following a bright idea, David began composing a non-fiction book on comparative religion with a visually distinctive side-by-side perspective of the legendary books, the Holy Bible and the Noble Koran.

The author lives and writes in the city of London.

Contents

Introduction

I've often wondered what would occur should the unstoppable force behind Christianity meet the immovable object that is Islam. Would the forces collide and shatter into pieces, merge into one, or merely destroy each other in a cosmic clash to end all days. There is only one way to be certain but I'd rather sit back and read a book than do my self harm or injury. The very best we can hope to do is to understand both sides of this great divide. Let us discover and fathom both the immovable and unstoppable.

Books of revelation are the most remarkable survivors. These very few books have overcome the endless wearing away of time, the bonfires of war, and the condemnation of the faithless, to remain highly revered and equally notorious. Not only to be read, studied, recited, and prized; these legendary books are inherited and thus signify a proportion of our birthright. Valued above all the clever books cluttering our wooden shelves and preserved in libraries and high security vaults are two ancient books which transcend the realms of standard print publications and world-wide sales. The Holy Bible and the Holy Koran have the support of nations and billions of devoted followers. With influence over domestic affairs and the capacity to sway global issues and strengthen acts of both war and peace. These two books of Holy Scripture are equally regarded as the greatest and most treasured compilation of the written word in human existence. This book offers a distinctive side-by-side perspective of the beliefs upheld by the Holy Bible and the Noble Koran. What remains undeniably unique is how the delivery of both viewpoints makes this perspective a very good read. When observing a standard coin we are not faced with both sides of that coin at the same time. The reading experience being offered here is based on the concept that when faced with both sides of a coin, at the very same time, the immediacy and awareness of the experience generates curios and fascinating results indeed; results worth talking about. This book presents just that with its quick and clever summations offering a visual and stylistic delivery that is immediate, fascinating, and free flowing. By all means a small book with a big idea.

Bible: **A Very Brief History**

The Bible is the first book ever printed, in 1454 A.D. and was originally composed in three languages: Hebrew, Aramaic, and Greek. It is a collection of sacred books and writings; consisting of the Old and New Testaments believed sacred by Christian religions and devoted world nations. The theme of the Bible is the redemption of humankind. The bible does not contain self-reference; the word 'Bible' never appears in the text. Since its launch the Bible has been translated into approximately 2,400 different languages and dialects. Also available in audio format for several non written languages and including an ongoing attempt to interpret the Bible into Klingon (a fictional language). Documented as the greatest best-seller of all published books with a remarkably high record of global sales, from an estimated 2.5 billion, to as high as 6 billion copies sold. Today the Bible is one of the most well-known books in existence. The Book consists of several genres of literature such as mythology, poetry, prophecy, narrative, letters, and sermonic literature. Inspired by God, this collection of records and written works was collected by men over a period of 1600 years (1450BC to 100AD). The progression of this great book covers more than forty generations and authors from all walks of life: from poets, scholars, kings, peasants, and philosophers, to fishermen, and statesmen. The writers lived under different circumstances and environments such as the vast wilderness, shadowy dungeons, and majestic palaces; across three continents: Asia, Africa, and Europe, during times of war, peace, poverty, prosperity, slavery, and freedom. The content of the Bible is read and understood to be God's instructions and revelations to the individual and the entire world. This book instructs Christians on how to relate to one another and those outside the church. It also reveals how its readers are to relate to God (Jehovah in Christianity). The average copy of the Bible holds approximately sixty six to seventy three books, divided into 1,189 chapters containing 31,173 verses and 773, 692 words. Copies are purchased, stolen, sold for profit, collected, presented as gifts, donated, discarded, recycled and destroyed.

Koran: **A Very Brief History**

The Koran is the only book in existence that is recited by millions of its readers as a requirement of their standard of living. Qur'an (pronounced 'Koran' because the letter 'Qaf' is not present in the English language), is the Scripture that declares God's religion as Islam; and refers to its follower as Muslim. The book is a work of dictation (God speaking to man), originally recorded in the Arabic language. The title means, 'that which is read' with its chapters arranged by size; larger chapters are revealed first. Muslims believe the Bible's true revelations have been distorted over time; the Koran exists to correct the Bibles discrepancies and reveal the unchanged word of God. This account of God's word makes the Koran the final Testament. The book has remained unaltered during its existence over 1400 years. Containing self reference, the word 'Qur'an' appears over seventy times in the book. The theme is the relationship that Allah (God) has with humanity. Since its launch the sacred writings have been translated into over 103 languages. Known as one of the great best-sellers an estimated 800 million copies have been sold and in Muslim households the Koran is the book which is most read. The Koran was revealed to the prophet Muhammad over a period of about 23 years. The word of Allah was memorized by Muhammad and passed unto his companions verbally; a process acknowledged as oral tradition. At the time of Muhammad's death in 632CE, the Koran did not exist as a written book. The writing and compiling of the text into the renowned book was accomplished by the first and third leaders of the Islamic community and completed around 650CE. For daily recitation the Koran is divided into thirty equal parts called paara; each part takes twenty-four reading minutes with the entire book requiring twelve reading hours. Average copies of the Koran contain approximately 604 pages divided into 114 chapters, 6,286 verses, and 99,464 words. Copies are purchased, stolen, sold for profit, collected, presented as gifts and donated. Believers do not discard or recycle the Koran with other paper. The usual means of disposal is for the book to be burned or buried.

Even Haleem's version says – "as corrected"!

Bible: **Within Touching Distance**

The Holy Bible can be found in homes, hospitals, hotel rooms, churches, schools, libraries, and book stores; not excluding military bases, cruise liners, clinics, law courts, museums, cathedrals, universities, town halls, marriage registries, prisons, and cemeteries. Copies are used in television stations, theatre and stage sets, Sunday schools and colleges, backpacks, shoulder bags, laptops, computers and smart phones. Allowing for the civic construction and layout of the typical western city; it can be speculated that a person is never more than thirty minutes away from a copy of the Holy Bible.

Koran: **Within Touching Distance**

The Koran applies the word 'Muslim' to humans, animals, and the inanimate world. The bird is a Muslim because it lives and dies obeying the sharia (the path that Allah has prescribed) for the community of birds. According to this Islamic thought all animals are Muslim. Allowing for the migration patterns of wild animals and the population of domesticated animals in towns and cities; it can be reckoned that a person is never more than 100 feet away from an animal obeying the sharia set out by Allah in the Holy Koran.

I shouldn't make clever remarks about heaven and hell. After all, when my time comes, I'll most likely have friends in both places.

SOURCE?

Chapter 1

The Creation of Earth and Everything

VERY FEW "REFERENCES" THROUGHOUT!

Bible: **A Matter of Days**

The creation of earth and all forms of life is disclosed in the first book of the Bible. The title Genesis is taken from its first verse and means 'beginning'. Genesis is the book of origins which describes the creation of the world by divine speech. The creation consists of eight commands executed over a period of six days: On the first day God created the light with the first sacred command. "Let there be light!" Luminosity and darkness are divided and the happening of day and night are named. The second command is spoken on the second day and created another divide, "Let a firmament be...!" This order triggered the separation of the waters above ground from the waters below. The firmament is named *skies*. On the third day two commands are spoken; the first calls for the waters below to be gathered together in one place and for dry land to appear. *Earth* and *sea* are named. The forth command instructs the earth to bring forth grass, plants, and fruit-bearing trees. On the fourth day the fifth command is spoken; glowing lights in the skies are created to signify the transition from day to night and reveal the time of day, the seasons, and years. Two great lights are also created: the greater light to govern the day and the dimmer light source at the night. The fifth day God commands the oceans to "teem with living creatures", and the birds to fly across the heavens with the sixth command. On the sixth day living creatures of all forms are brought forth with the seventh command. The eighth and final command initiates the creation of man; moulded from the earth (and woman from him). On the seventh day, having completed the heavens and the earth, God rests from work and sanctifies the seventh day. The entirety of this creation in sequence is described as "very good". The book of origins answers many of life's profound questions with reference to the beginning of life and the creation of everything. The author of the book of Genesis is not identified within the text, although it is believed to be work of Moses.

Koran: **A Matter of Days**

Accounts of the creation of earth and all forms of life that populate the earth are located within various chapters of the Koran. The subject of creation is split among many verses and is not presented as a singular, lengthy, and detailed narrative. In the Koran, reports of the first creation are set in context to remind its readers of the majesty and wisdom of Allah (God). Allah created the heavens, the earth, and all that is between both realms in six days. The Koran does not recount the stages of creation in any given sequence of events or in the manner in which Allah created the earth and its inhabitants. The verses that reveal the creation of the earth in six days use the Arabic word 'youm', which can mean 'one day' or 'one period in time'. After completing the creation of the earth in six 'youm', the Koran describes that Allah "settled Himself upon the throne". God does not rest on the seventh day. According to the holy texts Allah created the universe from a single entity; the skies and the earth were joined together as one unit of creation, after which, they were "cloved asunder". After commanding this entity to divide, the universe underwent a transformation into a cloud of smoke. It is from this cloud that Allah created the heavens and the earth. The very first earthly thing to be created was the 'noor' (light). From this light, and by Allah's authority and creative power, everything else was formed including all living things and mortal beings. The most eventful creation occurred when Allah moulded clay, earth, sand, and water into the shape of a man (woman created from this man soon after). The verses of the Koran dedicated to the creation of earth and everything answers a great deal of meaningful questions as to the origins of the universe and the divine power behind the elemental forces that created the earth and all living things.

Bible: **What's Mine is Yours**

"Let us make man in our image, after our likeness: and let them have dominion over the fish of the sea, and over the fowl of the air, and over the cattle, and over all the earth, and over every creeping thing that creepeth upon the earth." (Genesis 1: 26). It is written in the book of Genesis that humankind has the God-given authority over all the earth and the vast animal kingdom that inhabit the earth. Humanity was represented by the first human being Adam, who named all the livestock, the birds of the air, and the beasts of the field. He accepts the role of master and caretaker of the garden paradise Eden; the skies above, the oceans deep, and the entire world. "And the Lord God took the man, and put him into the Garden of Eden to dress it and to keep it." (Genesis 2: 15). Modern biblical interpretations do occasionally replace the word "dress" into 'tend' or 'cultivate', because to dress a thing is to embellish it and beautify it. As for the word "keep", this means to guard well something of value and maintain it soundly, and most importantly, to preserve and be faithful to it. With regards to all non-human life, after the great flood which consumed the earth, Noah (the arc builder) is given an idea of mankind's responsibility and the primal status quo. "…And the fear of you and the dread of you shall be on every beast of the earth, on every bird of the air, on all that move on the earth, and on all the fish of the sea. They are given into your hand" (Genesis 9: 1–2). Humankind has lead status above and beyond all other forms of life. With this supremacy comes the obligation to cultivate and preserve the earth's natural resources and subdue the wild kingdom of beasts. A caretaker's chief responsibilities are to preserve, guard, and be held accountable; to one day return the item of value to the owner in a satisfactory or improved condition than when it was received.

Koran: **What's Mine is Yours**

Mankind was created to represent Allah and to act as the appointed vicegerents on earth (persons chosen to exercise all or some of the authority of another). The Islamic term khalifah is the general word used to convey mankind's representative status. Man and woman possess divine authorization to populate, cultivate, and improve the earth. Humanity was destined to take up this role and so endowed with the knowledge required to accomplish the responsibilities of proprietor successfully. Adam and Eve fell victim to the evil persuasions of Satan and committed the first sin, after which, they repented and sought forgiveness. Following Allah's absolution the first man and woman were sent down to the earth to perform their roles as vicegerents of Allah with the promise of divine guidance. Those who followed the guidance would be rewarded. Whatever their different roles within society may be, men and women are bestowed with the position and accountability of Khalifah (vicegerent), thus forging the foundations of man and woman's essential equality as messengers of Allah. In Islam the role of khalifah carries three responsibilities: to be righteous, help others become righteous, and keep the earth uncorrupted, and beautiful. The belief that man is the representative of Allah has become so popular within the community of modern Muslim intellectuals and activists that when asked to offer an account of the most valued Islamic qualities, the description 'vicegerent of God', is almost certainly used.

SPELLING?

?

VICEREGENT ?

Bible: **Animals**

Animals perform key roles within biblical accounts of humankind's relationship with God and the earth. The human race is responsible for the survival of all earthly creatures. In the account of the eternal rainfall and resulting global flood, Noah and his family performed as the able bodied crew of the gigantic ark. The animals themselves were the passengers, the precious cargo. God reveals his love for the animal kingdom and our reliance upon them by ordering such a notable rescue. The human voyagers were eight in total; the numbers of animal species gathered in pairs were a hundred times more. The major distinction between human and animal is that the human being is created in the image of God, whilst the animal is not (Genesis 1: 26–27). To be created in the likeness of God means that one is like God and is therefore capable of spirituality, profound thoughts, sentimentality, willpower, and indeed the possession of an eternal soul. Animals do possess the living breath; however, they do not possess the eternal soul. The Bible names over 120 species of animals. From a religious viewpoint these animals are divided into two groups: the clean and the unclean. This is based according to whether the animals may be consumed or not. The Bible commands us to control the numbers of animals in general so that disease and sickness do not annihilate them. We are to use animals for our needs and subdue the beasts so they never bring harm to humans. Finally it is our responsibility to protect the animals from over-killing and abuse. In Genesis, God establishes the connection between the realm we occupy and that of the animal territories. It is good and right for a hunted animal to be eaten to feed the hungry. To put food on the table members of the human race can farm for foodstuff, buy foods, trade or hunt for food. The Scripture does not specify whether it is correct or incorrect to hunt animals for sport. The crossbreeding of wild animals to create a 'new' breed is frowned upon and it is considered acceptable, though debatable, that animals are used for pharmaceutical experiments and research. This is generally because the animals being tested upon serve as substitutes for the more precious human life.

Koran: **Animals**

There are over two hundred verses in the Koran that refer to animals and six of its chapters are named after animals. The Koran reveals that animals function as a community in the same way that human beings do. Animals praise and worship Allah through prayers, although this is not expressed in any form of comprehensible language to humans. "Each one knows its prayer and psalm, and Allah is aware of what they do." (Koran 22: 18). Passages in the Koran declare that all animals are endowed with spirit and mind. Furthermore the scriptures state that the consciousness of mind and spirit of an animal is indeed more than mere impulse and instinct. The word 'Muslim' is also applied to animals. For instance, a bee is a Muslim precisely because it lives and dies obeying the sharia (the 'way' or 'path') that Allah has prescribed for the community of bees. This is true of a person being a Muslim because he or she submits to the revealed *sharia* ordained for humans in the Koran. Mankind is to be held responsible for any injustice committed to any of Allah's creatures because every creature on earth has a share in all the natural resources. The kind treatment of animals is considered a good deed and the Koran calls for Muslims to treat all members of the animal kingdom with compassion and not abuse. Issues regarding experimentation on animals are grouped into three categories: The necessities without which life could not be sustained (al-Masalih ad-darurfyah). The needs vital for pain relief, distress and the improved quality of life (al-Masalih-al-haiya), and lastly, the comforts desired for enjoyment or self-indulgence (al-Masalih at tahsiniyah). Inciting animals to fight for game, pleasure, and profit is strictly forbidden in Islam. Also forbidden are the mutilation of animals without just reason, and the performing of unnecessary experiments in search of remedies for self-induced ailments. Islamic traditions employ humane slaughtering regulations by applying the least painful method to slaughter an animal. For example, the slaughtering instrument must not be sharpened in front of the animal and the slaughtering of one animal in front of another is prohibited. Prior to Islam, the ancient world had not practised such regard for animal life.

Bible: **The One and Only**

Christianity is one of the largest monotheist religions, which sanction the belief in a single, universal, all encompassing God. The term monotheism is applied particularly to Christianity, Islam, and Judaism. In practice Christians tend to emphasis the existence of one God that unifies the universe. "The Lord works in mysterious ways". Historically Christians believe that the nature of God is a mystery understood only through special revelation. There are over forty three passages in the Bible that proclaim the existence of a one and only God. Christianity does however embrace a belief that does not conform to Unitarian monotheistic beliefs. This unconventional belief asserts that God is reflected in three separate divine entities known as the Holy Trinity. In this instance God is one figure that exists in three eternal entities: the Father, the Son, and the Holy Spirit.

Koran: **The One and Only**

The belief in one God is a well defined characteristic of Islam, which views Allah, as the creator of all things. The supreme God watches over all human events and is the source of comfort, peace, and the highest sense of virtue, nobility and goodness. Islam is crystal clear in upholding the belief in one eternal, incomparable God. Only one God exists and the worship of idols is the greatest sin. Both Abraham in the Koran and Jeremiah in the Bible, dispute the act of worshiping idols created by human beings who possess the wisdom to create that which they decide to worship. The idea of a two-fold God is also rejected by the Koran (a powerful God of good and a powerful God of evil), and contends that both good and evil generate from Allah's creative act. Evil forces exist but do not possess the power to create. Allah is not a tribal, localised or provincial God but a universal God, an absolute divinity encompassing all affirmative principles.

It's better to stay quiet and to look intelligent, than to speak up and sound like a fool who should've kept quiet.

source?

Chapter 2

The Significant Others

Bible: **The Significance of Judas Iscariot**

The most ill-famed of Christ's twelve apostles is Judas Iscariot, son to Simon Iscariot, from the town of Kerioth. His name was common in ancient Palestine so the Gospel states his name in full to clarify whom the text is referring to. This apostle enjoyed a position of honour and was ever present at important occasions. Judas performed as the group's treasurer; he carried a money bag and made purchases for the disciples as needed. The apostle John states in the Gospel that Judas would every so often take for himself, from where the money was stored. Judas displayed the behaviour of a freethinker and cynic by choosing to address Jesus as 'rabbi' (teacher) not as lord. It was he who criticised Mary when she anointed Jesus with a precious ointment, the salve that he perceived as a source of income. Jesus gathered his disciples for a feast known as 'the last supper' where he mysteriously revealed that one of his disciples would betray him. All deny it, but Jesus seemed to know irrefutably that Judas would be the one to betray him. The awareness and surprising fore-knowledge of this betrayal has led many to believe that Judas Iscariot was indeed destined to betray Christ, as Jesus himself, was destined to die on the cross. Whether Judas's deeds were fated or not, his actions certainly contributed to the divine plan for the atonement between God and humankind. By playing such a key role leading up to the end of Christ and the beginning of Christ's legacy, the significance of Judas Iscariot, his friendship with Christ, his religious camaraderie, and his actions, are of remarkable importance to the life and death of Jesus. Following *the last supper,* Jesus found solitude in a remote garden. His prayer is interrupted when a band of armed soldiers of the high priest Caiaphas approached the area. Judas joins them and identified Jesus to the guards with a kiss. After a brief scuffle Jesus is seized. For his role in the successful capture, Judas was paid the sum of thirty pieces of silver. He commits suicide soon after the crucifixion of Christ. Judas has become the archetypal betrayer in western culture, with a role in virtually every piece of literature and art telling the 'passion' story. And a kiss from ones enemy or rival is still branded the Judas kiss.

Koran: **The Significance of Judas Iscariot**

The circumstances surrounding the whereabouts of Judas Iscariot on the day of the public crucifixion of Christ is of special interest to Islam. As indicated by the Islamic view, Judas Iscariot plays a vital role in the salvation of the Christian people. The Koran rejects Christ's crucifixion in light of a startling revelation. "…They did not slay him, neither crucified him, only a likeness of that was shown to them" (Koran: 4: 156). Islam teaches that Judas Iscariot was conceivably the victim of the crucifixion. Judas the thief and betrayer to Christians, is however to Muslims, the apostle who carried a great burden and died on the cross in a remarkable case of mistaken identity. It is believed that Judas was endowed with the physical likeness and appearance of Jesus. A resemblance so stunning that it deceived all the grieving onlookers, the capturers, and all of Christ's followers, including his mother Mary. "…They slew him not nor crucified him, but it appeared so unto them; and lo! Those who disagree concerning it are in doubt thereof; they have no knowledge thereof save pursuit of a conjecture; they slew him not for certain. But Allah took him up unto Himself". Supported by scripture there is unanimous agreement within the Muslim community in rejecting the crucifixion of Chris, in favour of what is generally known as the 'substitution of Christ'. Two equally enlightening perspectives about the substitution of Christ exist, namely, 'the volunteer' and 'the victim'. The first interpretation holds that Allah asked that a volunteer exchange places with Jesus. The volunteer's physical features were then transformed into the likeness of Jesus; to be persecuted and killed on earth whilst rewarded in paradise. The latter and reverse interpretation reveals that Allah used the substitution to punish the enemy of Jesus, and his traitor Judas Iscariot, was rightly chosen. Whether Christ was replaced with an unwilling Judas, or indeed a willing volunteer, what remains important is that the Koran states that Jesus Christ evaded the crucifixion and was most likely replaced by Judas Iscariot (Jesus ascended to heaven). This Islamic point of view makes Judas Iscariot, son of Simon Iscariot, perhaps the most significant of the twelve apostles of Christ.

So what happened to Jesus?

Bible: **The Significance of a Dead Man Walking**

Three people were resurrected by Jesus Christ: At first he restored to life the son of a penniless widow from Nain. He then revived the lifeless daughter of the Jewish leader Jairus. It is however his third resurrection that remains the most noteworthy. Lazarus of Bethania was brother to Martha and Mary; all were friends of Jesus. Following a plea from both sisters, Jesus visited Lazarus's tomb, and raised him from the state of death. Soon after this Lazarus took part in a banquet, which 'Simon the leper' gave to Jesus in Bethania. The raising of Lazarus is regarded as the most powerful of Christ's miracles because Lazarus was a corpse for four days. His body had begun to decay. There are accounts of other prophets who raised the dead shortly after death (Kings 17: 17–24), but it was Christ alone that raised a corpse in a state of decomposition. No other prophet had managed to reverse the state of death so far gone. Another astonishing account was that Christ displayed a startling power. Not in the resurrection itself but rather in the words spoken by the prophet Jesus. He commanded the miracle verbally using his own authority. He did not say 'I pray that God may raise you', but rather declared, "Lazarus, come forth". Prophets pray for miracles but on that day Jesus did not pray for a miracle; he spoke the words that commanded the dead to rise. He produced a miracle by the power and authority within him. This resurrection rendered many onlookers utterly speechless. Many Jews flocked to Bethania to see Lazarus and left believing in Jesus because of what they saw. The dead man that walked among the living was undeniable proof of the power in Christ. This miracle was a great threat to the religious leaders. The country was occupied by Roman military and both Jesus and Lazarus were becoming too popular; "If we leave him alone, all men will believe in him, and the Romans shall come and take away our nation" (John 11: 48). It's also written that, "The chief priests consulted that they might put Lazarus also to death" (John 12: 9–10). Lazarus vanished soon after the high priests ordered his death (last mentioned in John 12: 17). What became of him remains a total mystery. The resurrection of Lazarus was Christ's last miracle.

- except for His redemptive sacrifice/crucifixion
- and His resurrection!

Koran: **The Significance of a Dead Man Walking**

The Koran testifies that a prophet resurrected several dead people. These people were touched by a great healing power and miraculously brought back to life. The Holy book informs its readers that Jesus Christ was the prophet responsible, by the grace of Allah."...And you (Jesus) heal those born blind, and the lepers, by my leave, and behold! You bring forth the dead by my leave" (Koran: Sura Al-Ma'ida).

Bible: **Messenger of God**

In Christianity the archangel Gabriel serves as messenger of God. Biblical verses which specifically refer to Gabriel often depict this spiritual being as either mortal male or as being neither masculine nor feminine in physical characteristics. Gabriel first appears in the Book of Daniel and later (and most notably) in the Gospel. The angel is renowned for two specific visitations in particular where Gabriel foretells the births of two prophets, namely: John the Baptist, and his second cousin, Jesus of Nazareth. Regarding John the Baptist, it is written that an angel appeared to Zechariah foretelling the future; "Do not be afraid, Zechariah; your prayer has been heard. Your wife Elizabeth will bear you a son, and you are to call him John" (Luke 1: 13). The spirit identifies itself by announcing "I am Gabriel. I stand in the Presence of God, and I have been sent to speak to you and to tell you this good news" (Luke 1: 19). Shortly afterwards, Gabriel was sent by God to a small city of Galilee named Nazareth, where the archangel makes the most celebrated visitation. On this occasion Gabriel appears before a young virgin bride named Mary. "…Hail, you that are highly favoured, the Lord is with you: blessed are you among women" (Luke 1: 28). The New Testament speaks frequently of low and high ranking angels. The Bible contains not only visitations by archangels but also angels delivering holy messages, ministering to Jesus after his temptation in the wilderness, appearing to Christ in his agony, and again appearing at the site of his tomb after the resurrection. Angels also liberated the apostles Peter and Paul, from incarceration. In the biblical verses of the New Testament, sightings and events attended by angels are several; references to archangels however are much fewer in number, with only two references actually using the term 'archangel' (Jude 1: 9, 1 Thessalonians 4: 16).

Koran: **Messenger of God**

Al Malaikah (angels), are often referred to in the Koran. The belief in angels is a central factor of the Islamic faith based on the significance of angels in the Scripture. Angels are spiritual beings created by Allah to worship the creator and to perform specific duties within the realms of heaven and earth. In essence, they are the divine messengers of God. Within the dominion of angels there exists a celestial order of rank status consisting of the low ranking angels and the high ranking angels, namely, the angels and archangels. The chief angel Jibreel (Archangel Gabriel) is by far the most recognized angelic being in the Koran and within Islamic faith. Gabriel served as the intermediary through whom Allah communicated to many of the chosen prophets, revealing their obligations to them. Gabriel is most notably recognized as the chief angel that spoke often to the Prophet Muhammad, revealing the Koran to him over a period of two decades (twenty three years to be precise). Gabriel is also known as the 'spirit of truth' and the 'holy spirit' (not to be confused with the Christian meaning of the term). This archangel is the great messenger of God to a chosen few and chief of the four favoured and high ranking angels: Jibreel (Gabriel), Mikhail (Michael), Israfil (Raphael), and Azrael.

GABRIEL ≠ H.S.

Bible: **The Significance of Man**

There are over one thousand men mentioned in the Bible. The compilation of Holy Books was inspired by God and recorded by man. The first man to appear in the Bible is Adam; the one miraculously unique human being from whom we all descended. Adam was fashioned by the direct hand of God and differs from all other humans because he was not born of woman and so his body was without a navel (he did not develop in the womb). Adam set the standard for all humankind, he possessed the material (the flesh), and the immaterial (the soul). He was the first husband, the first farmer to the earth, and the first father to a child. By naming the different animals showed to him by God, he was also the first taxonomist. Adam is ill-famed for being the very first sinner which resulted in mankind's punishment to work through painful toil in order to prosper. Men and women are equal in regards to salvation; however in the traditions of Christianity, there is a leadership hierarchy established where men are viewed as cultivators to be *fruitful and multiply*. Men are also to subdue the earth because the world is a chaotic place. Traditional leaders of townships were male, similarly, Jesus chose twelve male disciples. As a servant of God the leadership role of man applies to his family and to roles within the church. The husband is responsible for labouring to provide for his family and must honour and love his wife devotedly. "He who loves his wife loves himself". Some proposed qualities of godly men are as follows: To be above reproach, a husband to one wife, self-controlled, respectable, hospitable, able to teach, not given to drunkenness or violence, and not a lover of money. He should set an example in speech, love, faith, and purity whilst displaying qualities of sensitivity and integrity. A man should also be a disciplinarian with children but not overbearing, quick-tempered, or pursuing dishonest gain. Many believe that the most significant tribute to Adams life was that God took from his body, one of his ribs, and from that rib formed another human being. And Adam said: "This is now bone of my bones, and flesh of my flesh; she shall be called 'woman', because she was taken out of Man".

Koran: **The Significance of Man**

The Koran is a work of dictation preserved by oral tradition and recorded by men. The first man is the masterpiece of Allah's creations and the first prophet of Islam. The story of Adam is mentioned twenty five times in the Koran. There is no account that man is created in God's image, and as for the first sin, the Koran places equal blame on both man and woman. The first man was created "from clay and mud moulded into shape". A bond that preserves the elemental attachment we have with the earth. It is also believed that the different colours of clay used in the creation accounts for the different skin tones of later people. In Islam, there is a social order established by Allah and His messenger Prophet Muhammad. This appoints man with the right of guardianship over the family unit in order to prevent friction between the spouses. A Man's role is to direct the household, feed his family, defend his home and lead in issues of politics, dispute and community issues. He must honour his parents (show particular care towards his mother); financially support them and his sister/s if unmarried. Within the family the son receives greater inheritance than the daughter because only the man carries the responsibility and burden of meeting all the financial needs of the family. Men are the managers, guardians of women; permitted to have up to four wives, but not commanded to do so. A man may marry a much younger woman, even prepubescent girls and endowed with the power to discipline his wife or sister by scolding or even beating her if necessary (if found guilty of immoral conduct. See Punishment of Wives, P 76–77). A man with many wives must provide separate living accommodation for each wife and divide his time equally among them. Contemplation and understanding should be part of a man's life. He must also cooperate with other Muslims in the defence of Islam and for the security of the Islamic nation. It is written that Adam grew lonely in Jannah (the Garden Paradise), and from his left rib, Allah created another. Allah then performed a nikah (marriage) between Adam and the woman. The Koran does not name the woman married to Adam, however she is known in Islamic tradition by the Arabic name Hawwa` (Eve).

Bible: **The Significance of Woman**

Woman is the only creation endowed with the natural ability to grow, nourish, and protect a human embryo internally; an impermanent quality of worth and significance in Christianity. Eve was a virgin at womanhood and for her share in committing the first sin womankind was sentenced to a life of subordination and the pain of childbirth. By tradition women were to mother the earth and wives required to be secondary to their husbands. Within the church supportive roles are entrusted to women and leadership roles to men. A passage in the book of Corinthians about women in church reads, "They are not allowed to speak, but must be in submission". Corinthians does however contain accounts of women prophesying in the church and does not condemn the act of free speech. Biblical scripture recounts marvellous reports of women departing from the custodial fabric of patriarchy. Women of the Bible proved themselves more than equal to the challenges and trials of their day. Several were considered touched by God and were full of faith, determination, and courage; there are stories of wives who defied husbands and even kings. In the book of Exodus, we find women in the roles of nursemaids or midwives using their powers to evade disastrous male politics. When the Pharaoh ordered the mass murder of all Hebrew infant boys, it was the daring and defiant acts of the Hebrew women that sustained the nation of Israel. Some proposed qualities of godly women are as follows: To be of noble character; trustworthy, reliable, creative, hard working, enterprising and charitable, organized, and of strong will. Whilst remaining dignified, wise, and fearing the Lord. She must be worthy of respect by displaying qualities of purity and self respect. Not addicted to wine, she should teach what is good, love her husband and children, and not be a malicious talker. The time of Jesus brought gender equality and end to female submission. Christ considered women equal to men and shared his teachings with women. After his crucifixion and resurrection, Jesus appeared first before his female followers, who were given the task of informing the others of the miraculous news. There are a total of 188 women named in the Bible.

Koran: **The significance of Woman**

Woman is the equal partner to man in the pursuit of knowledge, education and the procreation of humanity. Koran scripture condemns parents who feel embarrassed over the birth of a daughter. A key chapter in the Koran is based on Maryam (Mother of Jesus), who is among only eight honoured with a chapter bearing their name. In the Koran women are largely portrayed as kin to leaders and prophets, performing in roles within the home (as wife and mother). Women's rights are equal, but not identical, to the rights of men. This balance between 'duties' and 'rights' supports the person with more duties to perform in matters of finance and inheritance. "Women shall have rights similar to the rights against them, according to what is equitable; but man have a degree over them" (Koran 2: 228). The Koran obligation 'hijab' applies that both genders dress humbly and respectfully; a woman may cover all but her face and hands, or otherwise cover all but her eyes using clothing such as the burqas. Men are to cover themselves from the navel to the knees. Sharia law affirms that marriage cannot be forced on a woman and whether a man should take another wife is often based on the backing of his current wife, and this consent may be detailed in the marriage contract. No age limits are set for brides, e.g. Muhammad married young Aisha at age six. The Koran places no limits on travelling, under Islamic customs however; a wife may require the consent of her husband to leave the home for trips excluding her daily routine. With regards to auto travel, Saudi Arabia is the only nation where women are banned from driving cars. Some professed privileges of Muslim women are as follows: A woman is exempt from all financial liabilities; wives need not work or share in any of the family's expenses, household costs, and education fees. Mothers are supported by their sons. Unmarried daughters are supported by their fathers, and sisters without fathers are cared for by their brothers, and so on. Women are excused from some religious duties during menstrual periods (i.e. prayer and fasting). And a former wife may retain whatever she possessed before the marriage. Most of all, mothers enjoy a higher honour in the sight of Allah.

EXCEPT;
1 x WOMAN = ½ x MAN

I'm a very deep thinker. In fact, sometimes I think so hard and for so long, that I forget to think clearly.

Chapter 3

Great Expectations

Bible: **The Virgin**

Self control and personal integrity is a running theme in the Bible and Christianity allows for the expression of physical love within the respectable borders of marriage. Sexual union within marriage is deemed sacred because it is the deepest physical union possible. This union of husband and wife becoming 'one flesh' is the consummation of marriage; one that carries weight in building a meaningful spousal bond. Conception is the positive result of such an expressive union. Catholic Christians follow a pledge to abstain from sexual pleasures and engage in meaningful sexual unions only for the sake of procreation. A clear sign of virginity is not present in men. Circumcised Christian men undergo the cutting of the foreskin, which generates blood, and signifies a blood covenant between the man and God. Women have a particularly perceived physical sign of virginity (the hymen), which generally produces blood when disturbed. The presence of this blood provides the sexual union with the key element of oneness (the covenant of blood between the two people), a covenant that binds them. Virgins are highly valued, respected and desired. Virgin women signify purity and discipline. Christian women are encouraged to keep their virtue until marriage and the husbands are themselves directed to 'Love your wives, as Christ loved the church and gave himself up for her'. The Old Testament lays extreme emphasis on chastity before marriage and urges its readers to remain as virgin. Indeed the virgin birth of Christ in the New Testament upholds that principle that virginity is an important factor when selecting a mother figure based on virtue and devotion. In some cultures female virginity is closely interwoven with family honour. The loss of virginity signifies an end to innocence, the beginning of sexual maturity, and a rite of passage; a milestone in a young adult's personal life. In western terminology the word *virgin* is used to describe both human and non-human qualities. Fruit cocktails containing no alcohol are 'virgin cocktails'. Similarly, the purer and more valued 'virgin olive oil' is named so, for it contains no refined properties.

Koran: **The Virgin**

To remain a virgin until one is married is regarded a commitment and a duty. The Koran instructs its readers that the key to happiness in this life (and the afterlife) depends heavily upon how a person follows the laws of Allah, laid out in his book the Koran. Muslim sons and daughters are raised to believe in the value of virginity, and taught to preserve their chastity for their own happiness. The unmarried must keep themselves for their future spouses only and never permit the sexual advances or contact of anyone other than the person they are legally married to. Celibacy and virginity are promoted for men as well as women. "...And those who save their chastity. Except with their spouses and those whom they rightfully posses in wedlock, only then they will not be blamed" (Koran 23: 1–6). The Koran refers to the Virgin Mary a total of thirty four times, more than in the Holy Bible, with an entire chapter in honour of Maryam (Mary). The Koran text describes Maryam as a pious woman chosen by Allah above all other women. This recognition does well to signify the virgin bride as a woman of such compelling spiritual and worldly value to men and to God. Upon losing her virginity a woman may, in some cases, experience slight blood loss. This element serves as evidence of the virginity and is arguably what makes the virgin union recognized as a blood covenant that is binding. The cherished image and significance of virginity is fundamentally linked to purity, value, respect, charm, and the instinctive worth of a valuable thing (never been used), or a worthwhile spouse (never shared the blood covenant with another). In the Koran, the afterlife is portrayed as a peaceful and happy existence in the company of women and men of purity; A pledge that is available to all, not just the martyrs. Muslims are to maintain a very high level of conduct on this earth, and for the men, there is a very clear command. "Tell the believing men that they should lower their gazes and guard their sexual organs; that is purer for them...." (Koran 24: 30).

Bible: **The Whore**

According to conventional sexual behaviour and the length and breadth of erotic activity, promiscuity implies sex with many different partners. The term 'whore' however is associated with persons considered sexually shameless, morally loose, and most commonly, those who accept payment or valuable items in return for sexual favours. Outside the context of sexual deeds, a whore is a person who negotiates or compromises their principles for financial profit, personal gain, or an advance in social status. In the Bible the word *whore* is a noun; assigned to a person, place, thing, feature or action, and can function as the subject or object of a verb. It is hugely symbolic and deeply negative to be labelled a whore. The term is used in describing wayward people and nations with no sense of integrity and loyalty. Included are the individuals who humiliate, dishonour' and defile themselves. Along with the money lovers who sell their bodies, their talents, morals, and principles to the highest bidder. The Bible cautions against the bizarre and particularly those who whore themselves and encourage others to walk the line. It is also the Biblical train of thought that women have a heightened sexual influence over men. For this reason the female whore may wish to misuse her sexual influence to turn husbands away from their wives, and to set brother against brother. "To keep you from an evil woman and from the smooth talk of a loose woman" (Proverbs 6: 24). The great whore of Babylon is the Christian figure of evil and immorality; this prostitute is described as being "…drunken with the blood of saints and with the blood of martyrs of Jesus". This is the most potent symbol of the limitless power of whoredom. She is connected to the figures of the antichrist and the beast of revelations. This figure depicts just how the act of whoring (female or male) has been used to de-thrown kings, destroy families, devastate communities, and to ruin the lives of the poor, the impressionable and the unfulfilled. An account of the great whore is to be found in the book of revelations."The great whore that sitteth upon many waters…and the inhabitants of the earth have been made drunk with the wine of her fornication".

Koran: **The Whore**

To *whore* or commit whoredom is to indiscriminately sell or trade one's body, talents, and personal affections for a cash sum, valuable goods or social status. Adulterers live secret lives and the promiscuous enjoy sex with many partners, but only the whore lives a life that combines the elements of secrecy, with many sexual partners, and the willingness to sell to all who can afford it. Sex is a force of nature; no matter how many times you sell it, or give it away, it still belongs to you. Islam has a clearly defined moral code. Within this school of thought promiscuity, prostitution, whoring, and adultery are openly despised. Islam does not approve of the sexual activities, awareness, amusements, conduct or light-hearted sexual pursuits outside of the wholesomeness and integrity of married life. Being exposed to lust and promoting the notion of 'free sex' or 'sex for hire' puts a person in the undesirable and corrupt grouping of harlot, prostitute and whore. The term *whore* itself is not linked to the female gender in particular although it began as a female-only activity that flourished within a deeply contained and ancient profession with its own traditions of secrecy and the acquisition of wealth. Men who engage in sexual acts for money are also regarded as whores and male prostitutes. In Koran scripture the meaning behind the act of whoredom also involves the symbolic, emotional, and spiritual act of selling the body for some sort of personal gain. A person who seductively exposes their body or abuses their talents, and abilities, in a corrupt and shameful manner for the purpose of fortune and fame (which translates to profit), is indeed engaging in whoredom, and is a person of lesser character and worth. "The fornicator shall not marry any but a fornicatress or idolatress…" (Koran 24: 3).

Bible: **Call of Duty**

The term *Christian* means 'follower and believer of Jesus Christ'. There are certain principles that play a part in everyday Christian living. These values are taken directly from the Holy Bible and are not commands, but rather a set of wholesome, ethical, and moral values that champion the benefits of righteous living whilst remaining essentially linked to the celebrated Ten Commandments. The first is to *treat others as you would have them treat you*; without a doubt, the hallmark of Christianity. Biblical texts advise the reader to *have faith* and do not fret, because worrying does not add an hour to your life. *Help those in need* by visiting the unwell and donate to the hungry, those that require clothing, and the homeless. Get to *know the Bible* by making time for Bible reading. *Give thanks and be joyful* always and *pray* daily for your self and others. *Forgive your enemies* so that God may forgive you for the sins committed. *Be careful what you say,* because your words have the power to liberate you, and to the power to destroy you. And *learn the word of God* by reading the gospel: Mathew, Mark, Luke and John. It is estimated that with 10 to 20 minutes of daily reading a person can complete the four Gospels in a single month.

Koran: **Call of Duty**

There are five commitments to Islam that a Muslim must perform for the duration of their life. These compulsory obligations are recognized as the Five Pillars of Islam; collectively shaping the foundation of Muslim life. These commitments consist of *faith* (Shahadah), the declaration that there is no God but Allah, and that the prophet Muhammad is his messenger. Followed by *prayer* (Salat), five prayers conducted at particular times of the day whilst facing the holy city Mecca. *Charity* (zakah or zakat), allows for the more affluent Muslims to show concern for those in need and are required to make donations to provide support for the underprivileged in the local community. The fourth pillar of Islam is *fasting.* Muslims fast during Ramadan, the ninth month of the Islamic calendar and holiest period of the Islamic faith. The Fasting continues from sunrise to sunset and occupies one lunar month. The final principal is *pilgrimage* (Hajj in Arabic). During the hajj season, Muslims journey to the kingdom of Saudi Arabia where the holy city of Mecca is located. The physically weak or short of money are exempt from making the pilgrimage to the Makkah province however the physically and financially able, must make the hajj at least once in their lifetime. For Shia Muslims the pillars of Islam are more conceptual and seek deep contemplation, of which are; *Tawhid* (the unity with Allah), *Adl* (the divine justice of Allah), *Nubuwwah* (Prophet-hood), the *Imamah* (leadership of mankind), and lastly, the *Me'ad* (the Resurrection).

Bible: **Prayer**

The spiritual custom that strengthens the union between God and humankind through deliberate practice is known commonly as prayer. Prayer may be practiced anywhere and at anytime of the day, with variations in length, content, and structure (in words, song, or meditation). There are physical motions and sacred gestures that accompany the habitual prayer, such as, making the sign of the cross, kneeling, bows, and prostrations. Whilst the content of a prayer can be totally spontaneous or meticulously prescribed, there are some cast-iron closing statements that allow for a prayer's validity; standard closures include "through our Lord Jesus Christ", and "in the name of the Father, the Son, and the Holy Spirit". The most universally used closure is simply "Amen". These phrases serve as both affirmation and agreement between God and humankind. The Church exists in each of the 203 sovereign states of the world, of which the Catholic Church is the largest. The church serves as the meeting place for Christians to learn, share, help one another and pray. "The eye cannot say to the hand, I have no need of you", and neither can one deny the usefulness of the Church. Prayer is directed to God, although catholic and orthodox Christians do ask the righteous in heaven such as the Virgin Mary to pray on their behalf. Prayer remains at the heart of Christianity. The largest book of the Bible is the Book of Psalms, containing 150 religious songs often regarded as prayers. Perhaps the best-known Biblical prayer among Christians is 'The Lord's Prayer' (Matthew 6: 9–13, Luke 11: 2–4); A prayer chosen by Christ when he coached his disciples on how to pray. The main types of prayer are: *Praise and worship* (the most natural response to the creator), *thanksgiving* (reflecting gladness for life's blessings), *confession and forgiveness* (the admission of sin and plea for forgiveness), *meditation* (achieving stillness), and *supplication* (the Christian birthright to ask for all things great and small). The act of 'speaking in tongues' (or glossololia), hold no resemblance to any recorded language, but is deemed a Holy language by those who speak it. The authenticity of this form of prayer remains unconfirmed.

Koran: **Prayer**

Prayer is the dedicated act of directing ones gratitude, devotion, confession, and request to Allah. Prayer is one of the necessary practices of Muslim life. The importance of prayer is indicated by its status as one of the five pillars of Sunni Islam and part of the ten practices of Shi'a Islam. Muslims perform a brief ritualistic prayer (salah or salat), whilst facing the holy city of Mecca. The lifetime commitment to prayer is fulfilled five times a day under prescribed conditions. Performing salah is compulsory for all adult Muslims who have reached puberty and are sound of mind. Those in poor physical or mental health are allowed leniency with regards to prayer and physical posture. Tradition specifies that salah is to be performed five times a day, although the Holy Koran calls for the ritual to be performed three times a day, which are measured according to the solar movement of the sun. The five prescribed times for prayers are: near dawn (fajr), just after noon (dhuh), in the mid afternoon (asr), soon after sunset (maghrib), and around twilight (isha'a). Prayers may be shortened or merged and in some serious cases postponed. There are standard prayers (dua), recited for a variety of reasons such as after salah, or just before eating. A person may also say dua in their own words for any matter they seek to communicate with Allah. There is a well-known saying in Islam that 'purity is half the faith'. To achieve the appropriate and approved prayer, Muslims must be in a state of ritual purity; their surroundings and clothing should be clean and unsoiled, and for those menstruating or experiencing after-birth bleeding, salah is forbidden. For prayer, Muslims are required to cover their bodies in loose-fitting garments, and when praying in public both genders are generally separated to prevent distraction. Salah should be spoken in accurate, well pronounced Arabic. Failing to achieve the correct manner of speaking will nullify the prayer. The place of worship is the mosque, often referred to by its Arabic name 'masjid'. The removal of footwear is required before entering a mosque for prayer and most large mosques have towers where the call to prayer is performed.

Bible: **Religious Law**

Christian religious law consist of certain moral and ethical beliefs. There are many accounts for what is considered lawful within the faith. Religious law within Christian nations is not a required legal establishment with judicial powers and direct influence over common law, criminal law, civil rights, political issues, and national matters. However Christian religious law does on occasion have indirect influence over all of the above. Religious laws function largely within the Christian communities of churches, and in the personal lives of practicing Christians. The Ten Commandments are the universally accepted record of Biblical laws believed by most Christians as eternally binding. Laws can also be found in the Old Testament books. The instructions of Jesus Christ in the Gospel are also considered law, and referred to as the Law of Christ, or the New Covenant. There is also canon law (the internal body of rules) for the Catholic, Anglican, and Orthodox churches, and the laws found in the Pentateuch, the well-known Books of Moses.

Koran: **Religious Law**

[handwritten: NOT JUST "RELIGIOUS"]

Islamic law, otherwise known as sharia, is the most widely used religious decree and one of the three most common legal systems of the world; together with common law and civil law. Sharia law deals with many aspects of daily life including: economics, business, politics, banking, contractual transactions, family life, sexuality, social issues, and even hygiene. The origin of the word 'sharia' can be traced to the spoken Arabic noun *shari'a,* which appears once in the Holy Koran (45: 18). Sharia law varies from other religious laws because it derives many of its principles from juristic standards and reasoning by evaluation, (similar to the tradition of common law). Some particular laws are viewed as divinely appointed and everlasting for all relevant circumstances. These laws were formed by long established Islamic scholarship and are obeyed by most Muslim groups. In Muslim states, religious texts are law and Sharia is based on the Koran and the religion of Islam. Therefore Muslims have traditionally viewed Islamic law as essential to life. Sharia is the complete body of Islamic laws that regulate the public and private aspects of Muslim lives. According to Muslims, sharia law is founded on the teachings of Allah, and on the actions and instructions of the prophet Muhammad as found in the Koran. Sharia consists of four sources that Islamic legal experts refer to. The first two sources are the Koran and the Sunnah, (recorded deeds of Prophet Muhammad). The other two sources are consensus (Ijma) and comparison (Giyas). Sharia law may be divided into five key sections: The laws of worship and ceremony (Ibadah); which cover faith in Allah, prayers, fasts, charities and the pilgrimage to Mecca. The laws of transactions and agreements (Mu'amalat), comprising of all financial transactions, contractual agreements, endowments, inheritance, marriage, divorce, food and drink, child care, and also penal punishments, warfare and judicial matters. What follows are the laws of Morality and Behaviour (Adab), of values and beliefs (I'tiqadat), and last of all, the laws of punishments ('Uqubat).

Bible: **Forgiveness**

One of the most demanding issues a person may be called to cope with, is respond to wickedness, with kindness. This is a genuine act of faith that requires a profound grasp of morality and a great desire for peace. Forgiveness is the uppermost value needed in becoming, practising, and remaining a good Christian. The words 'forgiveness', 'forgive' and 'forgiven' appear 116 times in the Bible, with the main theme being that God is a forgiving God. In the New Testament, Jesus speaks of the importance of Christians forgiving one another and showing a great deal of mercy to others. Christians learn through scripture that forgiveness also comes with a heavy burden. "If you forgive men when they sin against you, your heavenly Father will also forgive you. But if you do not forgive men their sins, your Father will not forgive your sins." (Matthew 6: 14–16). Biblical texts also encourage a great deal of tolerance. "Bear with each other and forgive whatever grievances you may have against one another. Forgive as the Lord forgave you" (Colossians 3: 13). Forgiveness is a meaningful biblical concept. Since it goes against basic human nature, those who are willing to forgive do so by faith alone. Christians are urged and in some cases even pressured into learning the meaning of forgiveness and how forgiveness is closely related to a person's salvation. The books of the Bible consisting of the Old and New Testaments portray the image of an infinite and personal God that forgives every person who is truly remorseful of their sins and seeks forgiveness. Indeed Christianity is the only religion that offers the possibility of complete absolution. Forgiveness was the very last theme highlighted by Christ on the day of his crucifixion with his last spoken words. "Father, forgive them; for they know not what they do" (Luke 23: 34).

Koran: **Forgiveness**

Allah is most forgiving and remains the originating source of all forgiveness. In Islam, forgiveness often requires the repentance of those being forgiven, and forgiveness itself can come either directly from Allah, or from the person who was ill-treated. To comprehend divine forgiveness, a devoted belief in repentance is crucial. Forgiveness is earned only to those deserving of it and offered to those who plead sincerely to be forgiven. "Allah does not forgive idol worship (if maintained until death), and He forgives lesser offenses for whomever He wills" (Koran 4: 116). The Holy book goes on to clarify whenever possible, that it's better to forgive than to attack, and goes on to support this affirmation by portraying Muslims as people who "...Avoid gross sins and vice, and when angered they forgive" (Koran 42: 37). To receive forgiveness from Allah, there are three requirements to be met. The first; is to acknowledge the offense and its confession before Allah. The second is to make a sincere commitment not to repeat the offense. And the third is to ask Allah for forgiveness. A fourth stipulation is added if the wrongdoing was committed against another person or against society; to do whatever is necessary to rectify the offense (within limits), to make peace with the offended person and ask to be pardoned. Islamic teachings depict the Prophet Muhammad as someone who forgave others for their ignorance, even those who might have once considered themselves to be his enemies.

M. asked for forgiveness - a SINNER
Jesus did not   - not necessary!

Bible: **Code of Ethics**

Faith, kindness, and self-discipline are expected, respected and demanded. There's great emphasis on forgiveness over punishment. Idol worship and acts of wickedness are strictly condemned. Reading the bible and becoming familiar with the four books of the Gospel is very much encouraged. Fasting, regular prayer at home, and visits to the church for prayer, counsel, community gatherings, and donations are central to good living. Murder is a cardinal sin and adultery a great wrongdoing. The bible is strict in regards to human impulses and inward feelings. Jesus Christ raised the bar by stating that whoever lusts in their heart is guilty of adultery, and whoever hates someone is guilty of murder.

Koran: **Code of Ethics**

Sincerity and truthfulness are prized and very much appreciated. The consumption of some foods are condemned, most notably pork. Regular prayer and fasting are essential to the fabric of life. Idol worship and cold blooded murder are sternly condemned. The Koran should be read or recited often. Prayers should be performed facing Mecca. Pilgrimage to the holy city of Mecca is recommended to every Muslim. Most of Islam's laws, rules, and regulations are contained in the hadith (the words and practices of Prophet Muhammad), which specify punishments for men and women for the act of *zina* (premarital sex). Adultery is a direct violation of the marital contract and one of the major sins condemned by Allah. Punishment by stoning (rajm) is not stated in the Koran and based entirely upon hadith.

Some people have a rock-solid set of principles, and for a little money... well, they'll be more than happy to change them.

Chapter Four

Very Bad Things

Bible: **Adultery and Premarital Sex**

Western customs differentiate between the concepts of adultery (as sex between a married person and an unmarried person), and fornication (classified as sex between two unmarried people). In most European countries adultery (also known as sexual infidelity) is not a criminal offence and only becomes an officially recognized dispute when adultery has grounds for divorce under fault-based divorce laws. The deliberate act of adultery is considered by many Christians to be immoral and a sin. Of the well known Ten Commandments of God, it is the sixth commandment that declares "Thou shalt not commit adultery". There are many passages in the bible that uphold the belief in faithfulness with strong conviction.

"...the wicked will not inherit the kingdom of God? Do not be deceived: Neither the sexually immoral nor idolaters nor adulterers nor male prostitutes..." (1 Corinthians 6: 9).

With regards to a persons intentions of sexual desire, it is also written that "...Anyone who looks at a woman lustfully has already committed adultery with her in his heart" (Mathew 5: 28). Some churches have interpreted the act of adultery to include all sexual relationships outside of marriage, regardless of the matrimonial status of the people involved.

Koran: **Adultery and Premarital Sex**

Extramarital sex and premarital sex are known as 'zina' in Arabic. The phrase 'zina' signifies deliberate sexual relations between men and women not married to one another, regardless of whether one or both of them are married to other people. Therefore zina does not differentiate between 'adultery' (sex between a married person and an unmarried person) and 'fornication' (sex between two unmarried people). In the Koran, zina is one of the great sins besides murder and the belief in more than one true god. Sharia law imposes penalties for Muslim men and women upon committing zina because the law prohibits the act and considers this prohibition to be for the greater good and protection of all Muslims, for the integrity and preservation of matrimony. Adultery is a criminal offence in some Islamic countries. In Pakistan under the Hudood Ordinance, officials enforce the penalty of imprisonment and corporal punishment for adulterers. In cases of rape the issue has been particularly controversial because it requires women who claim to be victims of rape to provide extremely strong evidence to avoid being charged with adultery themselves. The most extreme consequence of zina is the sentencing and condemnation of some Muslim women and men to death by stoning (rajm). Perhaps only in Afghanistan, Iran, Nigeria, and the kingdom of Saudi Arabia, has the death penalty by stoning been performed. The stoning of a Muslim as punishment for sexual sin is not prescribed in the Koran itself, but is prescribed in the hadith (the teachings and activities of Prophet Muhammad); The Koran is the foundation of Islamic Law and the hadith functions as the explanation of those laws. There are prescribed punishments regarding illegal sexual activity in the Koran and many believe this to be noted in surah 24:2. "The woman and the man guilty of adultery or fornication, - flog each of them with a hundred stripes: let not compassion move you in their case, in a matter prescribed by Allah, if ye believe in Allah and the Lad Day: and let a party of believers witness their punishment". The legal standards of adultery do not apply in social and family disputes where the criteria for proof are not as rigorous.

Bible: **Sex with Animals**

Biblical passages about sexual encounters distinguish between holy unions and un-holy unions. Any kind of sexual activity between a member of the human race and that of the animal kingdom is considered an unholy union (acts of extreme evil, bizarre cruelty, and especially sinful conduct). The sexual involvement or enjoyment of a wild beast or domesticated animal is entirely forbidden. The Bible prohibits this sexual perversion and scripture warns against the coming together of human and beast with intense dislike."Do not have sexual relations with an animal and defile yourself with it..." (Leviticus 18: 23). The more severe biblical passages include, "Anyone who has sexual relations with an animal must be put to death." (Exodus 22: 19).

Koran: **Sex with Animals**

The Koran declares that a person should only engage in sexual fulfilment with the opposite sex in a respectable and lawful manner. Koran scripture does not expressly address the sexual union between members of the human race and those of the animal kingdom, however does suggest that any sexual activity should occur within members of a similar grouping. "And Allah has made for you mates (and wives) of your own kind" (Koran 16: 72).

Bible: **Homosexuality and the Sodomites**

Like all pursuits, sex involves the usual, and the unusual. When penetration involves an orifice not intended for sexual contact (such as the anus), the act is identified 'sodomy'.

The Bible is an advocate of wedlock and childbearing. One of the most cited passages in the book of Genesis is Gods approval for humankind to *be fruitful and multiply*. Following this divine, consent the most likely form of childbearing is through the sexual union of woman and man. The establishment of marriage within Christianity exists exclusively for the unification of man and woman, not for any other kind of union. In keeping with traditional beliefs, same-sex matrimony is improper because the purpose of marriage is to reproduce and only opposite-sex couples can naturally, without intervention of any kind, produce offspring. The Bible condemns all acts of sodomy, branding it unnatural, meaning; the union cannot bear children and deviates from the natural way of human breeding. There are few passages on gay opinions in biblical texts, with accounts of gay relations focusing only on the acts of sodomy and the consequences thereof. And what's more, the notion of sexual orientation is totally absent in the Bible. These exclusions exist for the very same reason that jet-planes and laptops are also absent in the Bible; because they did not exist in biblical times. The concept of sexual orientation is a 20th century outlook on sexual behaviour and certainly did not exist some thousands of years ago. Biblical passages on deviant sexual behaviour condemn the following: The rape of women and of men, prostitution (straight and gay); sex with non humans, sexually abusing children, and unions such as sodomy and bisexuality. The total destruction of the cities of Sodom and Gomorrah, play a major role in understanding the Christian view on sodomites. The Old Testament ties the destruction with two major events: the efforts by the men of Sodom to rape the visiting angels, and for their unfair treatment of widows, orphaned children, visitors, and the poor. All the same, it was the homosexual exploits of the inhabitants of the townships that Christians believe was the foremost motivator for their destruction by fire and brimstone.

Koran: **Homosexuality and the Sodomites**

The Arabic word for sodomy is 'liwat', under which the theme of homosexuality is found in most books of Islamic philosophy. Sodomy is a despicable act in Islam, more foul than adultery. It is forbidden for a man to engage in sodomy or allow himself to be sodomized. Husbands are not to sodomize their wives or engage in sexual contact anywhere that is not a place where something may 'grow'. The Koran speaks highly of matrimony and sexuality in Islam is, for the most part, lead by the Koran, Islamic traditions, and religious leaders. The universal consensus is that sexual intimacy should be confined to marital relationships between husbands and wives. On the subject of abnormal sexual behaviour, details of lesbian pursuits are absent in the Koran, whilst acts of sodomy are harshly condemned, deemed unnatural, and its practitioners regarded as acting senselessly and engaging in abominations. The characteristics of 'effeminate men' and 'masculine women' are common references used to identify gays in the Koran. The holy book recounts the kingdom of Sodom and its neighbouring city Gomorrah which were completely consumed by fire. In Islamic traditions the fall of both cities' serves as the proverbial expression of Allah's wrath against an entire township of sinners. The story of Lut (Lot in the bible), is reported in the Koran with slight variations, of which, the key distinction in the Koran rendition is that the total destruction of Sodom and Gomorrah was exclusively based on the homosexual and bisexual activities of the men of both cities. The men were engaged in sodomy with each other and also straight sex with their wives. Homosexuality under shariah law is a crime against God. The criminal aspect of gay conduct emanates from the Prophet Muhammad, considered to be the perfect example (Uswa Hasana). The Muslim majority in the East accept the harsh treatment of homosexuals as perfectly justified. The Prophet Muhammad himself stated "If you find anyone doing as Lut's people did, kill the one who does it, and the one to whom it is done".

Bible: **Murder**

When killing is deliberate and planned, it is considered murder. The commandment against murder is a cast-iron ruling for the preservation of Gods greatest creation, human life. To knowingly slaughter a human is to directly offend the creator. The commandment against murder is viewed by many Christian and non-Christian nations as a legal issue governing human relationships. Of the Ten Commandments revealed at Mount Sinai, the first five relate glaringly to man's sense of duty to God, whilst the concluding five commandments express mankind's obligation toward humanity. The New Testament bible maintains the position that murder is a moral evil; preserving the Old Testament view of bloodguilt (the guilt of shedding blood). Under the old Covenant, the Israelites were allowed to kill only under special circumstances such as warfare, the punishment of sins, i.e. murder (Exodus 21: 12–14), and even adultery (Leviticus 20: 10, Deuteronomy 22:22–24). Because murder is the unlawful taking of human life, the New Testament acknowledges the role of civil government in maintaining justice and penalizing evildoers to the point of capital punishment, thus legitimizing laws such as the death penalty for heinous crimes and atrocities and by validating acts of self defence and legal warfare. Killing is handled differently to murder in the Bible. The book recognizes that a person might accidently kill another or that people may kill to protect innocent lives. *The sixth commandment (thou shalt not kill) does not* include accidental killing, self defence, acts of legitimate warfare or capital punishment, but is rather about the deliberate and unjust killing, that is, murder. The catholic catechism instructs that human life is sacred and no one has the right to claim or destroy an innocent human being. Catholic teaching prohibits euthanasia and abortion because these killings are premeditated and destroy innocent human life (falling under the catholic definition of murder). Readers of the New Testament are generally raised to believe that every act that endangers human life is disapproved of, whether it arises from carelessness, wantonness, or from the cardinal sins.

Koran: **Murder**

Chapter four in the noble Koran contains verses that inform readers not to kill, commit murder, or suicide. Deliberate acts of killing and of suicide are forbidden. The Koran also expresses the safeguarding of infant life by commanding Muslims not to kill children (Koran 6: 140, 17: 31), under this ruling abortion is also regarded a form of murder. Islamic law authorizes the Koran ruling that one may take human life only "by way of justice and law." This decree legalizes the death penalty which in Islamic nations is often applied by the court as punishment for the most nefarious crimes. Islamic policy on criminal penalty holds that severe punishment functions as a deterrent to serious offenses that destroy individual lives and threaten law abiding communities. The following crimes are in some cases punishable by death: premeditated murder, rape, adultery, terrorism, piracy, acts of homosexuality, and the spreading of mischief such as treason (*fasad fil-ardh*). In times of war, Muslims are commanded by the Koran to protect themselves through defensive battle, against clashes from enemy armed forces. Under these circumstances killing is permitted and not considered murder. Verses that promote battle and combating in the Koran do so within the context of warfare. The common quotation, or rather, misquotation of the 'sura 9: 5' continues to stir controversy as it is regularly used outside of the context of warfare, battle, and oppression.

"Once the Sacred Months are past, (and they refuse to make peace) you may kill the idol worshipers when you encounter them, punish them, and resist every move they make. If they repent and observe the Contact Prayers and give the obligatory charity, you shall let them go".

The decision to defend or attack is justified in cases of war and oppression, and the killings are validated by Allah. "...If anyone kills a person - unless it be for murder or for spreading mischief in the land - it would be as if he killed all people. And if anyone saves a life, it would be as if he saved the life of all people" (Koran 5: 32). — *Misquoted.*

& what about 9:29 ?

Bible: **Witchcraft**

The paranormal or supernatural powers of a person used to benefit others (for healing purposes), or to inflict harm and otherwise influence nature through occult means, is known as witchcraft. The phrase witchcraft is used as a blanket term for both the evil and the good forces of witchery. The general practitioners of witchcraft are commonly known as witches and wizards. Some powerful witches and wizards are able to consult with and summon spirits. This is achieved by feeding, rewarding, entertaining, and making pledges with the spirits in exchange for the knowledge of charms, curses, fetish rituals, and spells. In Christianity, the act of sorcery is associated with heresy and is viewed as wicked and immoral. Indeed many Christians believe that Christianity is still engaged in a secret battle against Satan and the army of demons, wizards and witches. According to this view, witches still go to cross-roads and to burial sites and cemeteries to call on the wicked and the monstrous spirits of the dead. The most characteristic quality of witchery is the ability to cast spells; through the use of worded incantations, and the performing of physical rituals such as animal sacrifices, the consumption of bizarre herbs, and the use of amulets and potions. Mirrors, swords, and bones of dead animals make up the standard tools of the occult trade; a trade which also demands spiritual commitment. A person cannot serve two masters, therefore the categories of witchcraft and sorcery described in the Bible, ward off and protect its readers against the forces of witchcraft. The general authority is that Christians should have an unconditional allegiance to God and should therefore make no contact with, or make allegiances to, the various forms of witchcraft and sorcery available. The New Testament acknowledges that witchcraft and magic does exist, but it is forbidden to practice witchery on the basis that it usually involves the worship of other gods. All forms of the occult practices such as hypnotism, magic, necromancy, fortune telling, and astrology, are forbidden by God and the New Testament condemns the custom of witchcraft as an abomination.

Koran: **Witchcraft**

Summoning mystical powers through sorcery and witchcraft with the intent of influencing, domineering, deceiving, and inciting conflicts, is a force that Muslims are familiar with as witchcraft exists in Islam. The power of sorcery stems from the old world of pagan gods, covenants with spirits and the manipulation of the elements around us; these paranormal forces are real, and as old as the trees.

"But the Shaitans disbelieved, they taught men sorcery". "…men learned from these two, magic by which they might cause a separation between a man and his wife; and they cannot hurt with it any one except with Allah's permission, and they learned what harmed them and did not profit them, and certainly they know that he who bought it should have no share of good in the hereafter and evil was the price for which they sold their souls…" (Koran 2: 102).

The Koran is a book of power. Its ancient scripture is endowed with the authority to protect and defend its believers. Different sections of the holy book offer different effects upon the reader; from positive and uplifting, to protection and the defence against forces of witchcraft. According to various customs, the prophet Muhammad was, on one occasion, targeted by sorcerers and managed to annul the negative effects of the mysterious paranormal attack, through the recitation of the appropriate verses of the Koran to attain victory.

Many of the food and drink on offer can dull and corrupt the mind. It's not wise to rely on your judgement when your senses are out of focus.

Chapter 5

*Food and Drink
and What Comes After*

Bible: **Food and Drink**

"Food is for the stomach and the stomach is for food" (Corinthians 6: 13). Food and drink communicate numerous messages in the Bible and indicate developments in scripture. Food restrictions are not to be confused with sins, but rather a guide to eating well. The forbidden fruit consumed in the Garden of Eden, represents the vulnerability we all share when we choose to eat strange foods or devour substances that are offered to us. At the time of fasting Christians refrain from eating any or little food in order to attain spiritual nourishment. In the Bible, food is used to convey symbolic messages to the reader. Meat is always at the centre of good meals and festive banquets and is a sign of being well fed. Food offerings are usually meat based and accompanied by a grain offering and a drink offering; preferably wine, but in some cases beer. Barley is one of the most important foods in the Bible and consumed as porridge mainly. Wheat is more valued and baked into bread. The highly valued fruits include olives and dates; a good source of energy. Vegetables, beans, fruits and herbs and spices were abundant in biblical times and very well used. No restrictions apply to the consumption of plants. Animals however are divided into three groups: animals on land, creatures in the water, and birds in the sky. Traditionally animals were considered to be clean or unclean. The eating of horses, cockroaches, birds of prey, swine, animal fat, and the drinking of animal blood were all unhealthy practices in the Old Testament. However the prophet Peter, in a vision, is scolded by God and commanded to no longer label Gods creations unclean. In modern Biblical texts all food is declared clean. The best-known food related events are instantly recognizable in art and popular culture. The 'last supper' presents an everlasting image of how friends and enemies break bread together. The 'feeding of the five thousand' represents the importance of staple foods and how thousands can be unified or divided by their access to the most basic foods. A Christian practice is to pray before every meal to bless the meal and express thankfulness to God.

Koran: **Food and Drink**

It is noted in the Holy Koran that honey is the best of all edible foods, and milk is the drink most favoured due to its natural wholesomeness. The Prophet Muhammad, along with his companions, survived on the simplest of foods; never giving in to excess or a heavy diet consisting of rich foods. During the time of *Ramadan* (a *month* of obligatory daily *fasting* in Islam), abstention from food is closely related to moral and spiritual progress. Aside from fasting, prophets reach a high spiritual and moral rank by eating very little, and eating only the simplest foods, thereby maintaining a heightened spiritual mindset. Foods permitted under Islamic dietary guidelines are called 'halal' foods; the phrase *halal* meaning permissible or allowed. Prohibited foods and ingredients are called *haram* (forbidden). In order to make meat permissible (halal), the meat or poultry must have been slaughtered in a ritual manner known as zibah. According to the dietary guidelines gathered from the Koran, Muslim followers cannot engage in the following gastronomic activities: The consumption of animals not slaughtered in the name of Allah, and of carnivorous beasts. The consumption of pork or pork by products, and of the meat from an animal that died prior to it being slaughtered for food; the intake of blood and blood by products, consumption of birds of prey, drinking of alcohol, consumption of land animals without external ears, devouring meats sacrificed on stone alters or in the name of a lesser God. The prohibition of certain foods is simply a measure to safeguard human health. However if a Muslim person is forced to eat any of the forbidden foods out of necessity i.e. hunger, starvation, extreme poverty, et cetera, the conduct is forgiven by Allah. A well known Islamic tradition is to pray before meals in order to bless the meal and convey thankfulness to Allah.

Bible: **Music**

Music appears throughout the Bibles Old and New Testament. There are over 1,150 verses in the Bible that make references related to music. The use of music in the worship of God, while at church or in the home, has undeniable biblical support. The Bible does not forbid music and singing. The Holy books contain music, song, and hymns which are heartfelt means of communicating and connecting with the lord God and Jesus Christ. Music is recognised as a means for praise, and expression of joy, thanksgiving, sorrow, and spiritual communication. There are no absolute divisions between praise (which is sung) and prayer (which is spoken). The Book of Psalms speaks often about praising the Lord with song. In the New Testament, the act of singing hymns serve as a source of great comfort and strength. Jesus Christ sang hymns with his disciples, with one of the most famed occasions taking place after the Last Supper. The role of music in worship continues today. Many church services begin with a song of worship because music is a universal and international language that we all share. Music also helps Christians to focus on the messages in the Bible, the stories in the scripture, and the word of God. Above all, just as the musicians of the biblical era once did, the modern day Christian uses music to exalt the name of God. The Bible describes worship as "pleasing" to God, and a requirement of those who follow Christ. Melodious worship is uplifting and can touch the soul. Countless people are moved to tears during musical worship, whether in the church, with other Christians, or alone.

Koran: **Music**

It is highly debatable among Muslims whether or not music is considered haram (forbidden) or halal (permissible). This difference of opinion is largely based on how the Koran texts are interpreted. It is considered that a Muslim who follows the Koran accurately will not find any such prohibition whatsoever of music or singing contained in its scriptures. Allah's commands are very clear regarding any prohibition given in the Koran so many believe that the prohibition of music and singing cannot be found in the Koran, because Allah does not prohibit them. Music is one of the purest and most beautiful creations of Allah, who set the tone and rhythm of every sound in the universe. Music and singing are therefore like all the creations of God that constitute an important part of our daily life. Any prohibition of music or singing is believed to be influenced by Islamic laws and the books of hadith and sunna. The books of hadith and sunna were written over 200 years after the death of the Prophet Mohammad. Many believers openly state that these books occasionally contradict the Koran, as the Prophet Mohammad himself followed and preached only from the Koran. In Islamic nations the enjoyment and appreciation of music is a subject that has been actively debated by top scholars. Many of these scholars have been generally inclined to condemn all forms of music, with the exception of the ad-duff (tambourine), played at weddings. Quite a few respected scholars have taken a positive approach to the tolerance of music and singing, considering only the music containing sensual, pagan, or unethical themes and subliminal messages as categorically forbidden. Koran reading is the reading aloud, reciting or the chanting of sections in the Koran. It is not considered music by Muslims and when recited the style is structurally dissimilar from music. Koran reading may be based on one to three vocal tones only. Similarly, each melodic passage centres on a single tone level, but the melodic contour and melodic passages themselves are largely shaped by the reading laws.

Bible: **Alcohol**

There is more scripture condemning the use of alcoholic beverages, than on the subjects of lying, adultery, cheating, hypocrisy, pride, and blasphemy. Jesus Christ's first miracle was changing the water at the wedding of Cana in Galilee, into wine. He transformed between 120 and 180 gallons of water into wine. However Jesus did not create, utilize, praise, or command his disciples to use intoxicating wine. The Bible does not forbid the drinking of beers, wines, or indeed any other drink containing alcohol, but does speak harshly, about becoming enslaved to drink, especially to the point of drunkenness. Drinking alcohol can become addictive and Christians are not allowed to engage in acts that might encourage sin, and influence others to sin against their conscience. To tempt, encourage, provoke or pressure others to drink excessively is out of the question. In light of these principles, it would be extremely difficult for any Christian to say he or she is drinking alcohol excessively, to the glory of God. "Wine is a mocker and beer a brawler; whoever is led astray by them is not wise" (Proverbs 20: 1). The New Testament advises its readers not to get drunk with wine. Elders and deacons should not be addicted to wine or strong drink. Older women who serve as role models to the younger ones must not be addicted to wine. Men are dissuaded from sitting with a woman and drinking wine greatly. Wine is not considered the same as grape juice in the Bible, because if it were, the Bible would hardly condemn the abuse of fruit juice. The biblical take on alcohol is really quite straight forward: it is an issue of moderation. The general contours of biblical teachings are that wine is something to be enjoyed, and like any good thing, it can be abused. Christians are to avoid drunkenness, not avoid alcohol; discipline not denial. Verses that show approval of grape wine speak about the unfermented grape wine (juice), whilst verses that expose the evils of wine, allude to the intoxicating fermented wine. The Church of America took a stance for total abstinence in the 1920's resulting in the great prohibition era of American history, during which, alcohol for consumption was banned. The prohibition amendment was revoked thirteen years later.

Koran: **Alcohol**

The prohibition of alcohol appears in several separate verses in the Koran, and revealed at different times. At first, it is forbidden for Muslims to attend to prayers whilst intoxicated. A later verse reveals that alcohol contains some good qualities and some evil qualities as well, however the evil is greater than the good. Finally scripture declares that intoxicants and games of chance are 'abominations of Satan's handiwork'. The verses within the Koran that forbid intoxicating substances are interpreted by Muslims with no exception to the type of intoxicating liquids available; covering the fermented, distilled, and brewed alcoholic drinks. Over the years, the list of intoxicating substances has come to include modern street drugs and the like. It is also understood that "if it intoxicates in a large amount, it is forbidden even in a small amount." For this reason, some Muslims avoid alcohol totally, even minute amounts used in cooking. According to Koran and Sunnah (practices and traditions of the Prophet Muhammad), there is a curse attached to the ten people in connection with wine. These include: The wine presser, the wine manufacturer, the wine taster, the person who transports wine; the person to whom it is transported, the wine server, the wine seller, the merchant who profits from wine, the person who buys wine, and the one for whom it is bought. The purpose of the Koran warnings against intoxicants is to emphasize to Muslims that purity of mind is essential to achieve spiritual progress. Alcohol is the source of many individual and social ills and sinful behaviour. Shariah law looks to the Koran as its foundation for every prescriptive and proscriptive direction for Muslims. It is against shariah to buy or sell grapes for the purpose of making wine and all forms of commerce that involves wine. Actions may also be taken to curb drunkenness, for instance, if a relative returns to the home drunk, the Muslim men of the household may give him forty lashes for it. Although the Koran bans the use of alcohol in this life, the book goes on to describe rivers of wine that flow through paradise in the after-life. Based on passages in the Koran, it is generally agreed that in paradise, wine does not cause intoxication.

Bible: **Greed**

Greed is as old as the gospel. The biblical view on how to cope with greed is unambiguous and contains one of the most legendary quotations about the endless desire for money and material things. "The Love of money is the root of all evil" (Timothy 6: 10). The love of money and wealth, covered under 'greed', is one of the cardinal sins; a classification of the most objectionable moral weaknesses. If left unchecked, greed can develop into a fixation that can never be satisfied. In the pursuit of success and riches it is possible for some to become blinded by their greed and use deception, fraud, and lies to acquire more material goods, at the expense of others. Biblical passages caution against materialism, the friendship of those who profit from the greed of others, and those who forever desire what others possess.

Koran: **Greed**

The Koran blesses charity and teaches that greed is against the will of Allah. Merchants, vendors, and sellers are commanded to be honest and display generosity. Greed is an undesirable habit that leads to various sins. Most of all, greed is the selfish and excessive desire for material wealth, money, food, and other worldly possessions, especially when the desired goods are available only to the privileged. It is believed that a mind occupied with thoughts of greed cannot unfold the divine meaning of the Holy Koran. Greed may be limitless, and if not controlled, can function as a great distraction, persistently diverting a person's attention away from the true purpose of life. Islam requests that tight fisted persons embrace generosity with the hope of attaining something better in the afterlife. During the fasting period of Ramadan, Muslims set a firm limit on their eating, smoking, and sexual activity; it is believed that this abstention develops a heightened moral standard which helps to curb a persons potential for greed, extravagance, and other vices. The fourth pillar of Islam is almsgiving: making voluntary contributions to the poor and disabled as an act of worship. 'Zakah' is the Islamic principle of offering a percentage of one's earnings to charity or the distribution of finances for the same purpose. This custom is also regarded as purification from greed.

Bible: **Lust**

Lust is an intense sexual desire. The Bible teaches its readers and followers that surrendering to lust is a worldly hunger beset with destructive results. Conceding to sexual lust can lead to some negative sexual impulses, urges, and sexual misconduct. This includes, but not limited to, sexual addiction and dependency, infidelity, incest, distasteful sexual perversions, bestiality and rape. Lust is a selfish transgression that functions only to please one's self in a sexual capacity; a decision which leads to unwholesome sexual pursuits and desires with no consideration to the consequences. There are many forms of lust and the bible differentiates between the three main kinds:

"For all that is in the world, the lust of the flesh, and the lust of the eyes, and the pride of life, is not of the Father, but is of the world." (John 2: 16).

The Bible is an advocate of moral values and good righteous living, and therefore lust, is a shameful and dishonourable sin.

"Any other sin that a person commits is outside his body, but the person who sins sexually, sins against his own body" (Corinthians: 6: 18).

Koran: **Lust**

Lust is a passionate, or overwhelming sexual desire. According to Islam, human desires and cravings are a part of natural life and cannot be ignored. Therefore Muslims must learn to master the strengths and weaknesses within. If a person fails to do so, he or she then becomes a servant to their appetites and consequently fall below the level of animals. In Islam, it is believed that Lust is a blind driving force and must never be allowed to become the driving force of Islamic society. When lust overcomes a person, they become self centred, viewing love as a means of self gratification; a selfish wrongdoing. A person can be affected by lust at any age and the Islamic tradition enlightens Muslim men and women on the many ways to curtail their lustful desires: "Whenever a man is alone with a woman, Satan is the third among them." When a couple are together, they should be supervised and the woman is to dress modestly. A man should curb his desires during adolescence so that he is accustomed to controlling these desires during adulthood. Islamic tradition has established certain bylaws to curb lustful activities: Under these laws, Islam forbids listening to the female voice with lust and desire. Secondly, the women of Islam are to wear veils; the purpose of the veil is so the woman is dressed in a manner that may not excite men to feel sexual desire or to lust for her. Furthermore, women are not to display 'fineries, ornaments or beauties' of their female form, as this may awaken a man's lust. What's more, women are not to speak softly to men, or in a way that might excite men to lust after them.

"If you fear Allah, then do not be soft in speech, lest he in whose heart is disease should covet, but speak with appropriate speech." (Koran 33: 32).

Passages in the Koran encourage modesty for both genders and the Islamic religion calls for chastity in all factors of life.

Bible: **Sloth and Laziness**

Slothfulness is the failure to utilize one's skill, natural abilities, and God given talents. Laziness is a sin based on neglect than action. The slothful and the lazy are wasteful because they squander their years unproductively; by not achieving, learning, working, or creating. The result is a wasted life due to the lack of purpose and usefulness. A person displaying slothful qualities harbours great indifference and misplaced priorities, with a tendency to avoid responsibility and meaningful relationships that require hard work. Slothful behaviour may cause Christians to neglect their faith and to develop a spiritual lack of interest; by neglecting the word of God, the wisdom of Jesus Christ, and the solace of the gospel. The antidote for sloth is passion and enthusiasm. Christianity offers a solution for slothful existence, and that is to know God, read the Bible and to realize your purpose and capacity to do some good and help others, find love and know happiness. "The soul of the sluggard craves and gets nothing, while the soul of the diligent is richly supplied" (Proverbs 13: 4).

Koran: **Sloth and Laziness**

Slothfulness and laziness are together a sign, or perhaps even a warning that something is very wrong, a physical symptom of a spiritual imbalance. The reluctance to work or exert oneself in any way, shape or form is a capital sin. Those who overcome slothfulness will surely rise up and find rewards for their hard work. Plenty of rest and relaxation is permissible in Islam, yet moderation is needed because a lazy lifestyle keeps the body, the mind and the spirit from fulfilling obligations and realizing aspirations. The Koran values of honour and morals are attained through optimism, and enthusiasm. Performing good deeds is only possible when a person is free of apathy and indifference and sluggishness. This ethical viewpoint is one way of receiving a peaceful and positive outcome in the Hereafter (the spiritual afterlife). When a person shows laziness in prayer or is indifferent to prayer, that person breaks the spiritual attachment to God set by religion. What follows is a life lacking a key element to attaining personal wellbeing, spiritual fulfilment, wholesomeness, and the great value of belonging. Islamic remedies to combat laziness include prayers that help Muslims turn to Allah in supplication and to seek help in fighting sloth and laziness.

Bible: **Vanity**

Vanity is rumoured among writers of fiction to be the devils favourite sin and allied with immortality, physical perfection, youth and vitality; a well-known and preferred offering of demons and witches in their quest to convert the vulnerable, the gullible and the faithless. Whether or not vanity is indeed the devils favourite sin is irrelevant in this case, what's more, proving such a claim would take some skill. Vanity is not treated differently from other kinds of transgressions and its capacity to encourage larceny, abuse authority and wealth, and acts of selfishness, greed, self-harm, envy and violence. An enduring sense of vanity may grow and intensify over time due to an over-developed sense of egoism and pride. Vanity may be identified as 'the excessive belief in one's own attractiveness to others'. The vain at heart cannot function without receiving the full attention of those around them and often engage in all that is humanly possible to preserve that status and remain the centre of attention. Vanity in western art and sculpture is often symbolized by a peacock in parade; flaunting its dazzling array of brightly coloured feathers, or by a nude woman facing a large mirror. The mirror is occasionally held by a demon. Most of the biblical references to vanity appear in the Old Testament books. In the New Testament vanity is characterised by the Whore of Babylon. In orthodox churches, vanity makes up one of the eight sinful and diabolical sins which every Orthodox Christian must refuse to give in to. Vanity is considered a form of self worship. To Christians in particular it is a form of self worship, where one rejects God for the sake of one's own image and in so doing become separated from the graces of God. The stories of Lucifer (Satan) concentrate on a spiteful and destructive aspect of vanity.

Koran: **Vanity**

The essential quality of vanity is the way in which a person thinks particularly highly of themselves on account of some advantage gained (real or imagined). The vain generally perceive others as inferior to them due to an obvious physical strength or beauty, financial supremacy, recognition or influence earned or possessed by them. A great number of traditions point out the destructive effects of vanity with varying degrees of caution because vanity is indeed a great motivator. *"And eat not up your property among yourselves in vanity"* (Koran 2: 188). The Koran declares that Muslims should not walk the earth with pride and vanity and goes on to list the damaging side effects or by-products of vanity which are, but not limited to: arrogance; self worship, an overblown sense of value, the negligence of one's errors and failure to resolve them, ungratefulness (for God's blessings), a selective memory and belief in opinions that suit them only. There is a proverb in Islam taken from the Koran that explains what may arise should a man deeply contemplate his modest beginnings as a drop of sperm, his certain end as a handful of dust, and the brief interval of his life; He will forget his vanity and devote his entire life to the worship of Allah.

Perish man! How unthankful he is! Of what did He create him? Of a sperm-drop. He created him, and proportioned him, then the way eased for him, then makes him to die, and buries him; then, when He wills, He raises him (Koran 80: 17–22).

The opposite of vanity is modesty; a worthy trait that leads to the edification and spiritual growth of the human soul. It is therefore necessary for Muslims to turn to Allah and to know Him. The realization that only the all-powerful Allah deserves worship and praise is a good starting point in accepting that vanity is a form of self worship, and worship should be directed only to Allah.

Bible: **Masturbation**

Masturbation is the physical stimulation of ones genitals to the point of orgasm. Otherwise known as 'solo sex', this act is frequent in humans of all ages and is entirely legal, given that its not performed in public places, which could fall under law enforcement rules on indecent exposure and lewd conduct. It's alleged that masturbation is beneficial to the body's reproductive system because the human body may masturbate naturally; this occurrence is known as a 'wet dream'. In females wet dreams can provide protection against cervical infections by increasing the acidity of the cervical mucus and by moving debris out of the cervix. In males the wet dream expels old sperm with low motility from the genital tract so that the next ejaculate will contain more active sperm with higher chances of achieving conception. Wet dreams are called 'nocturnal emissions' in the Bible and scripture does not directly label masturbation a sin. Christianity however associates masturbation with the indecent and sometimes wrongful thoughts and images that accompany the act. Many conservative religious groups regard masturbation as an offence against chastity and brand it a sinful practice. These beliefs are based on a number of Old Testament laws called 'uncleanness'. Under the old law, any time a man ejaculated he became unclean for the day; anything his semen touched also became unclean. Leviticus speaks of ejaculation in general but doesn't specify the cause.

"…And if any man's seed of copulation go out from him, then he shall wash all his flesh in water, and be unclean until the evening" (Leviticus 15: 16).

The Old Testament describes the death of Onan, who many orthodox Christians believe was killed because he masturbated. Further analysis of the passage revealed another interpretation which indicates that Onan was punished for using a primitive method of birth control. Latter-day Christian churches generally accept the second interpretation and no longer use the term Onanism in reference to this nocturnal activity.

Koran: **Masturbation**

Masturbation is the most common form of sexual self gratification. There is no direct reference to masturbation in the Koran and thoughts on the sexual act are largely based on hadith, Islamic traditions and cultural attitudes. Unlike sexual contact with a spouse (which is approved of), masturbation is generally a sexual act performed alone, and by the unmarried. For the un-married, masturbation is a cultural taboo in the Shia, Sunni, and all other associated Islamic subdivisions. Islam makes it very clear that sexual acts outside of marriage are prohibited according to the Koran. Many consider ejaculation, regardless of the cause, as ritually impure. When fasting, during Ramadan or other times, a man is considered to have broken his fast if he ejaculated on purpose, either through masturbation or intercourse; and upon ejaculating must not pray, hold a copy of the Koran or enter a mosque, until he performs 'ghusl' (the washing and cleansing of the body required for various rituals and prayers). The ritual cleansing of the body after sexual intercourse and or sexual discharge is compulsory for adult Muslims. Wet dreams are treated somewhat differently however because the person is asleep when it occurs. The requirement for wet dreams is that the person is to bathe prior to undergoing any of the rituals necessary for Muslim daily living.

Adulthood has opened my eyes to the reality that for some people, sexual intimacy involves a beautiful stranger, a warm bed, and a cash transaction.

Chapter 6

Sins on a Daily Basis

Bible: **The Multiplication of Sins**

The human conscience is our intuitive sense of right and wrong; functioning to approve or disapprove of our actions. The conscience persuades us to behave within the limits of an existing moral code and virtuous conduct upheld by what a person believes in, in this case, the Christian faith. Nevertheless, the conscience is very much like a muscle which strengthens only if exercised regularly; if the muscle is not tested and strained, it will weaken over time. For the times when our moral boundaries are weakened and resistance to sin is at a low, the human spirit will commit and accumulate sins by the minute. Christians view the concept of sin as a wrongdoing of the religious or moral laws set by God and recorded in the Bible, especially if this wrongdoing is deliberate. The intentional fulfilment of a sin is a sign of disobedience to the divine will of God, and can result in the spiritual separation from God. A sin can be dishonourable, offensive or totally immoral, and is not necessarily associated with committing a wrongful deed, but also by failing to commit a rightful endeavour as well. Essentially, sin is the rebellion against, or resistance to the direction of God, and the hostility towards the good and the righteous. In Catholicism, a sin may be categorized as either mortal or venial. A mortal sin is one that is grave in nature and committed knowingly and deliberately and thus in defiance of God's will. A venial sin lacks the gravity of a mortal sin and results from the ignorance of God's law, or is not performed willingly or purposely. Estimating the rate at which the average person may 'sin' in a single day is a matter of dispute. In western cultures it's alleged that the daily, widespread sins committed by people of all ages, creed and ethnicity, are to be found in the Christian classification of general wrongdoings known as 'cardinal sins': pride, envy, greed, lust, wrath, gluttony, and sloth. This category of vices has been employed since the earliest of Christian times to educate and enlighten its believers on the human tendency to sin.

Koran: **The Multiplication of Sins**

The human nature has many qualities. Each of these virtues and traits has the potential to benefit humanity and therefore the human nature is fundamentally good. Nonetheless human beings do have the ability to sin largely and without end. The human conscience is the instinctive way of recognising transgressions based upon a person's moral code, in this case, the Islamic faith, and making the right choices to curb sinful behaviour and to live a righteous life. A sin is an act, exploit or deed that is contrary to the will of Allah. Human beings are to worship and serve Allah. Islam is the submission to the will of Allah, and following the commandments of Allah is the meaning of Islam. If a person disregards the will of Allah and deliberately acts against these wishes, then the person is committing a sin. There are seven major sins in Islamic tradition called the 'pernicious seven' or 'deadly seven', based on hadith. These seven sins are considered kaba'ir (meaning the great or major one's), and is used to indicate the serious evils and severe wrongdoings.

"Avoid the seven noxious things: associating anything with Allah, magic, killing one whom Allah has declared inviolate without a just case, consuming the property of an orphan, devouring usury, turning back when the army advances, and slandering chaste women who are believers but indiscreet."

Many religious clerics and public speakers point out that Islam's major sins are greater in number based on the definition of major sins as 'acts which are clearly forbidden in the Holy Koran', by 'the Prophet Muhammad', and for which there is a '*hadd* punishment' (penalty specified in the Koran). Based on the above definitions the list of major sins can be up to 70 in total. Minor sins are acts which are displeasing to Allah but for which no specific punishment or strict caution has been issued.

Bible: **Money**

"A feast is made for laughter, and wine maketh merry: but money answereth all things" (Ecclesiastes 10: 19).

Even in ancient times it was clear that the power of money made many things possible through trade, purchase and bribe. The origins of the well used proverb 'money is the root of all evil' can to be found in biblical passages. The Bibles stance on 'money' applies to every society and trade industry, and whilst money itself is not sinful, the love of money is the cause of many evils which have been known to influence the decisions of individuals, families, and entire nations. A person who single-mindedly accumulates money and wealth is likely to neglect family, friendships, and even their personal safety.

"No one can serve two masters. Either he will hate the one and love the other, or he will be devoted to the one and despise the other. You cannot serve both God and Money." (Matthew 6: 24).

The following ideals are the 4 main biblical principles to the administration of one's money and riches: The first principal covers the payment of taxes. Jesus Christ was known to endorse the government's right to taxation. "Render to Caesar what is Caesar's, and to God the things that are God's". The second covers the tithe, which is, one-tenth of ones earnings or proceeds that is paid as a voluntary contribution to the local church. The third principle for the administration of money is to keep some money aside for savings; parents are to save for their children's upbringing and to provide for their households during emergencies. The final principle is to live within the means of ones income; "Owe no man anything", and do not allow yourself to be overrun with debt. Many of the great riches paraded in public may well be the proceeds of dishonest and immoral businesses.

"Better to have little, with godliness, than to be rich and dishonest." (Proverbs 16:8)

Koran: **Money**

The word 'money' appears five times in the Koran (verse four - Shakir translation); however the appropriate management of ones money is revealed in greater detail, spanning more verses. The following Koran principles are applied to the administration of money, wealth, and capital resources: In the area of commerce, interest and loans, the Koran forbids the practice of taking exorbitant or excessive interest. In Arabic there's a clear distinction between interest (fa'eda) and excessive interest (Reba). The Koran forbids Reba. With regards to charity, it is compulsory to collect 2.5% of one's income each year and have it donated to the poor. Every so often this donation is mandatory when a certain amount of one's earnings is exceeded. Within savings and inheritance, it's the duty of a Muslim man who has something of value to prepare an Islamic will regarding it (called al-wasiyya). An heir is never deprived of their inheritance. In business, all proceeds must be acquired legally. It is even proclaimed that 'The truthful and trustworthy businessman will be in the company of prophets, saints and martyrs on the Day of Judgment'. Bribery is also prohibited and considered a wrongful endeavour while misers are warned not to withhold their money, 'lest Allah withholds from you'. Muslims are encouraged to spend what they can and spend on others…so Allah will spend on them. No extravagance or pride should be implicated with what a Muslim does. The Koran advises its readers to desist from squandering their wealth and refers to Christians and Jews as those who consume their wealth irresponsibly.

"Lo! Many of the (Jewish) rabbis and the (Christian) monks devour the wealth of mankind wantonly and debar men from the way of Allah." (Koran 9: 34).

Bible: **Pornography**

Pornographic media remains one the most popular topics explored in bookshops, video rental stores, and viewed on the internet. The visual impact and addictive quality of pornography is recognized as a source of corruption. Christians feel that pornographic images possess the power to obscure the concept of sexual reality to adolescents, corrupt the innocent, and abuse the recklessness of youth. Pornography is a medium used to exploit those prone to making extreme choices. It has been established by law enforcement departments in the U.S.A. that pornography and the porn industry have certain ties with organised crime, drug abuse, and the manipulation of the under-aged, underprivileged, unhappy, and the weak minded. The three main categories of sin are; the lust of the flesh, the lust of the eyes, and the pride of life. Pornography is a lust for flesh, whilst exhibiting itself through a lust of the eyes. Lusting after someone in your mind is considered offensive in the Christian faith, therefore practicing Christians take sensible steps to reduce their exposure to graphic sexual content."Will you defile yourselves the way your fathers did and lust after their vile images?" (Ezekiel 20: 30). Pornography was not well established or widespread during the time of Christ. Christians look to the Gospel of Mathew for the biblical view on viewing a person lustfully.

"Do not commit adultery. But I tell you that anyone who looks at a woman lustfully has already committed adultery with her in his heart". (Matthew 5: 27–28).

Churches habitually discourage members of their congregation from any exposure to pornography. Some influential Christian churches support government legislation to restrict the publication and distribution of pornographic materials.

Koran: **Pornography**

Pornography may be considered as un-Islamic. Koran passages forbid all actions that are indecent and scandalous. The general Islamic thought on pornography essentially refers to the vulgar, obscene, shameful, indecent, and foul aspects of porn. Watching pornography is a form of expressing ones desire for sexual relations and of physical sexual contact. Islamic customs have high regard for marriage. Matrimony is very well respected and recommended in Islamic customs and communities world-wide. It is suggested that young people marry, especially if they have sexual desires and therefore fulfil those sexual desires in a proper and worthy manner, leading to a happy and healthy sex life that may lead to the formation of a family. Pornographic imagery and motion pictures are prohibited within the Muslim faith. In some cases the public display of affection between two adults may be chastised by the law enforcement officials if their actions are deemed as improper. The Islamic solution to living in a society where pornographic images are widespread and easily available is to lower one's gaze.

"Tell the believing women to lower their gaze and keep covered their private parts, and that they should not show-off their beauty except what is apparent, and let them cast their shawls over their cleavage. And let them not show off their beauty except to their husbands. (Koran 24: 31).

It may surprise non-Muslims to learn that viewing porn can be a form of adultery in Islam. To observe an unmarried couple having sex, is to take pleasure in watching them commit 'Zina' (sex outside of marriage), which itself is haram (forbidden).

Bible: **The Punishment of Wives**

The responsibilities of a Christian man and husband does not include the punishment of his wife. There are no passages in the sacred books of the Bible relating to the discipline of wives by their husbands.

Koran: **The Punishment of Wives**

The Koran maintains that a husband may, in some cases, discipline his wife or wives. The fourth chapter of the Koran, surat al-Nisa' (women), contains a few passages that are understood to prescribe the female subordination to husbands in particular. The verses in question (Koran 4: 34), have become notorious.

"Men are the maintainers of women because Allah has made some of them to excel others and because they spend out of their property; the good women are therefore obedient, guarding the unseen as Allah has guarded; and (as to) those on whose part you fear desertion, admonish them, and leave them alone in the sleeping-places and beat them; then if they obey you, do not seek a way against them; surely Allah is High, Great" (M.H. Shakir interpretation).

Many have defended the phrase 'beat' in the scripture to mean 'lash'. The general idea was to have the unruly woman shamed rather than physically harmed. Others however believe that the 'beatings' are physical but only to be performed if the wife has become guilty of some openly immoral conduct, whilst some men simply follow the teachings precisely to the letter. It is the use of the Arabic term 'waidriboohunna' that causes the debate. According to the Lane Lexicon (page 1779), arguably the best Arabic-English dictionary, the term *waidriboohunna,* means to 'beat them'. Several respected translators of the Holy Koran have interpreted the word *waidriboohunna* with varying results: The following are five interpretations by highly respected translators:

And last, beat them (lightly): Yusuf Ali interpretation.

And beat them: Arberry interpretation.

And scourge them: Rodwell interpretation.

(And last) beat them (lightly, if it is useful): Al-Hilali/Khan inter.

And beat them: M.H. Shakir interpretation.

It has taken twenty years for me to understand that having a long day with nothing to do is a delightful pleasure for young children, but having the very same thing, is frustration for the old.

Chapter 7

Life is for Living and Dying

Bible: **Gluttony**

Gluttony is the over consumption of food and drink to the point of physical discomfort or waste. The sin of gluttony is quite easily overlooked as a severe wrongdoing. People tend to associate sins with deliberate acts that are committed out of character, and toward other people. This is not the case with gluttony which by all accounts is a daily and habitual sin that can become part of ones standard of living, daily routine, and lifestyle choice that is passed on to children. Over-indulgence may even be considered a sign of wealth and privilege. Gluttony possesses destructive properties; when confined to eating, the person can develop physical deceases, disorders, and emotional pain over time. Gluttony is essentially a sin of which one exists to please themselves; connecting this act to selfishness, a lack of self discipline, and wastefulness. Biblical passages about self discipline preach that we must have control over our appetites and to never allow our appetites power over us. If we are powerless to manage our eating habits, then it is fair to assume, that we may have difficulty controlling other lifestyle behaviours. Medieval church leaders took a more expansive view of gluttony and went as far as to prepare a list of six ways to commit gluttony; which included: *nimis* (eating too much), *praepropere* (eating too soon), *laute* (eating too expensively), *studiose* (eating too daintily, out of vanity and leaving some to waste), *ardenter* (eating too eagerly, to the point of burning), and *forente* (eating wildly). It is understood that gluttony makes one sluggish and drowsy; this may foster laziness and possibly lead to another of the seven deadly sins.

Koran: **Gluttony**

Gluttony is the over consumption of food to the point of waste. It is not considered an actual sin in the Koran; however, the Prophet Muhammad advised his companions and wives not to overindulge. Islam sets effectual laws to protect health and body from illness, corruption, and filth. Gluttony is not permissible as it may lead to illness and is frowned upon in order to ensure good health and wellbeing for the body and for the soul. The fasting of Ramadan is a meaningful period of reflection over past deeds and self-reformation; a period which also develops discipline, tolerance, the urge to do good, and also to improve one's health by discontinuing any reliance on rich foods and other forms of gluttony.

"O Children of Adam! Wear your beautiful apparel at every time and place of prayer: eat and drink: But waste not by excess, for Allah loveth not the wasters" (Koran 7: 31).

RAMADAN is NOT a true FAST. It is simply a re-scheduling of meals from day time to night time.

Bible: **Inter-Racial Marriages**

Having in a romantic relationship or a deep emotional connection based on love and affection with a person of another racial group is classified quite simply as interracial dating. Interracial dating is no different from any other kind of dating and does on many occasions lead to marriage and the bearing of multiracial children. The Bible informs its readers that we are all of one blood (Acts 17: 26). We are all the descendants of Adam and Eve, and of Noah after them, therefore we are all members of a single race, universally known as the human race. In the New Testament Christians are commanded not to marry unbelievers. Race is not an issue. The Holy Bible denounces marriages where one spouse worships God and the other is an active unbeliever or idol worshipper. When selecting a suitable companion for marriage Christians are urged not to accept or offer any preferential treatment based on race. The person's good nature, faith in God, and Christ are the biblical standards for choosing a spouse. Scripture forbids inter-religious not interracial. The Old Testament Law (in Deuteronomy) commanded the Israelites not to engage in interracial marriage. The reasoning behind this instruction was based on the view that people of other races at the time engaged in idol worship. "For they will turn your sons away from following me…" The book of Exodus discloses that when Israel left Egypt, a mixed multitude of people moved with them and explains that a stranger may not eat of the Passover, however if the stranger converts to the faith, and in the case of many men, become circumcised (a symbol of spiritual conversion), the stranger shall then be accepted. "He shall be as a native of the land… One law shall be for the native-born and for the stranger…" (Exodus 12: 48–49). It is also worthwhile to note that Moses, who was raised in Egypt, married Zipporah, a woman identified as an Ethiopian (Numbers 12: 1). Zipporah was accepted because her religion was true and her father Jethro worshipped the one true God.

Koran: **Inter-racial Marriages**

Interracial marriages are welcomed in Islam and endorsed by many influential Islamic prophets, tribal leaders, and scholars. A Muslim man, if he so wishes, can find love and happiness with a Christian or Jewish woman provided they live within the guidelines of Muslim family life. During the period of pre-Islamic Arabia (known as the Jahiliyyah era), spiritual leaders including the Prophet Muhammad Ibn Abdullah fought against tribal discrimination within the society he lived in and promoted interracial marriages, using the Koran to support his aim of unity.

"O mankind! We created you from a single (pair) of a male and a female, and made you into nations and tribes, that ye may know each other (not that ye may despise (each other). Verily the most honoured of you in the sight of Allah is (he who is) the most righteous of you. And Allah has full knowledge and is well acquainted (with all things)." (Koran 49: 13)

Many Islamic tribes, villages, and large bordering territories use interracial marriages to break down the barriers of intolerance and to unite Muslims. The marrying of non-Muslim women from foreign nations was a common association that contributed to the growth of Islam within non-Islamic regions and nations with historical significance. From the 9th century a large number of mostly male Arab merchants and buyers from the Middle East inhabited and settled in the Malay Peninsula and Malay Archipelago. They traded with and befriended the Malay peoples and intermarried with the local Malay, Indonesian, and Filipina female populations, resulting in the spread of Islam in Southeast Asia. It was also common for Arab conquerors and explorers to marry local females in the lands they conquered within various parts of the world and especially Africa. When it comes to interracial marriages the Islamic and Koran viewpoint is both undemanding and culturally aware. Muslims are encouraged to set aside all ethnic and ancestral differences and to first and foremost exist and coexist as Muslims.

Bible: **Male Circumcision**

The term circumcision means to 'cut around'. The circumcision procedure involves the removal of the foreskin around the penis by cutting along the top of the foreskin, clamping the skin, and separating it from the penis. Biblical circumcision is a physical and instantly recognizable expression that a male has favoured to live his life for God and is in control of his own body. It is practiced as a religious rite found in the Abrahamic Covenant and is therefore practiced by Jews, Muslims, and some Christians (most prevalent in the Jewish and Muslim faiths). Male circumcision generally occurs shortly after birth, during childhood or around puberty as part of a rite of passage. The majority of Christians no longer practice circumcision under Old Testament laws and the circumcision ceremony is no longer a necessary ritual. This is revealed in a number of New Testament passages. These verses proclaim that the reliance upon Christ's finished work on the cross makes Christians 'circumcised of heart' and so the circumcision of the flesh accomplishes nothing.

"For in Christ Jesus neither circumcision nor uncircumcision has any value. The only thing that counts is faith expressing itself through love" (Galatians 5: 6).

The First Church Council in Jerusalem declared that male circumcision was no longer necessary in modern Christianity. The subject is still divided amongst the churches with many Christian religious organizations remaining neutral about biblical male circumcision. Even so, the ritual is still customary among the Coptic, Ethiopian, and Eritrean Orthodox Churches and many other African churches. Male circumcision was once a requirement for gentiles to convert to Judaism but the leaders of the Christian Church at the Council of Jerusalem have rejected the ritual as a requirement for conversion. This obligation for circumcision was possibly the very first act of differentiation of early Christianity from its Jewish roots.

Koran: **Male Circumcision**

The foreskin removed during circumcision is a layer of skin with no apparent indications of where the skin should be cut during the procedure and so the measure of foreskin removed can vary differently. For that reason no two circumcisions are the same. The origin of circumcision in Islam is a matter of religious and scholarly debate because it is not mentioned in the Holy Koran and many are split on whether the circumcision ritual is optional or essential. Circumcision is however mentioned in Hadith (the teachings and actions of the Prophet Muhammad and his companions), and regardless of the fact that it doesn't appear in the Koran, is widely practiced among Islamic peoples and is most often considered to be a sunnah, a holy tradition. The validation of the circumcision of Muslim males is based on Ibrahim's covenant with God. Part of the religion of Ibrahim is the performing of circumcisions.

"Then we inspired you: 'Follow the religion of Ibrahim, the upright in Faith" (Koran 16: 123).

The Koran deals extensively with Prophet Ibrahim; his name is mentioned sixty-seven times in the book, but nothing of him being circumcised. This offers a reason as to why there is no consensus on whether circumcision is indeed optional or necessary. The timing and location of Muslim circumcisions vary from hospital settings to the home, and from a few days after birth, to between the ages of six and eleven. The event is celebrated with sweets or a feast, and considered an important celebration in a male's life. Male circumcision is among the rites of Islam and is part of the 'Fitrah', or the innate disposition and natural character of the human creation.

Bible: **Female Circumcision**   — *NOT CHRISTIAN!*

Practitioners of the circumcision of females consider it to be an integral part of their cultural and tribal identity. Some practitioners and their participants also associate the ceremony to religious obligation. Some African rural communities and close-knit religious groups do insist on the practice of female circumcisions at present; these tribes, predominantly illiterate, and the religious leaders within these communities, include members of the Christian faith. The Holy Bible makes no mention of female circumcision. The act of female circumcision itself is not declared explicitly, neither does the Bible state the requirement of females to be circumcised or include any such passages naming any women, or particular women of influence who were themselves circumcised, endorsed or encouraged the circumcision of females in any way.

Koran: **Female Circumcision**

Female circumcision, which is the partial or entire removal of the external female genitalia by cutting, has indeed been practiced for centuries. The precise origin of the ceremony is unknown and is said to predate Islam. In some countries such as Egypt, female circumcision is practised by Muslims, yet the act is not recognized in the majority of Muslim nations, leading to the conclusion that female circumcision may be associated with cultural practices and not the religion of Islam. There are no instructions in the Koran scripture that calls for Muslim men or women to engage in any form of female circumcision. Passages of the Holy Koran do not contain any indication of female circumcision having been performed. Believers of the ceremony do not support their beliefs with verses from the Koran but refer instead to a particular hadith (reports of the activities of Prophet Muhammad), which appears to accept the act of female circumcision.

"Circumcision is a commendable act for men (sunnah) and an honourable thing for women (Makromah)". (Al-shawkani, Nayl Al-awtar, Dar Al-Jeel. Beirut. 1973. Vol. 1).

Many respectable hadith scholars consider this hadith to be of uncertain and insubstantial legitimacy. The Holy Koran contains no indication or statement of female circumcision.

When you feel hatred, you may contain it inside you until the time comes to unleash it upon your enemies. But remember one thing; hatred is a vicious acid that burns whatever holds it and destroys the vessel from the inside.

Chapter 8

The Untouchables

Bible: **The Virgin Birth**

The terms 'virgin birth' and 'virgin conception' are common in Christianity. The spiritual conception of Jesus Christ is revealed in several ways. Two are most noted: whilst one validates the conception by placing emphasis on Mary's husband Joseph, who "Knew her not till she brought forth her firstborn son". The other is the visitation of angles to a number of people in preparation for the birth. Mary was visited in Nazareth by the angel Gabriel during her engagement to Joseph and was informed of her divine purpose and approaching pregnancy with the assurance that; *"Nothing will be impossible with God".* A priest and his wife (Zacharias and Elizabeth) were paid a visit by a divine messenger. Zacharias was informed by the angel that his wife would give birth to a son named John (the Baptist), and this man would prepare the way for Christ. Both the immaterial element (the Holy Spirit) and the material elements (the vessel and the womb) were united to make the miracle conception a possibility. The child born to Mary was the personification of the spiritual and the physical. In Christian traditions the nature of sin is passed down from generation to generation. Because Christ was conceived through a sinless union, he was the only person to be born without sin. The New Testament Bible holds four accounts covering the life of the man born of virgin. Each account has a different style of coverage and separate degree of focus. These four books are commonly known as 'the gospels'. The accounts of Mark and John begin with the baptism of Jesus by John the Baptist, with the reports of Mathew and Luke, opening with the miracle birth and genealogy of Jesus. It is the latter two gospels which provide the only canonical accounts of the birth of Christ and clearly report the view that Christ was conceived without sexual union, but rather, was the result of a miracle birth brought about by the Holy Spirit.

Christians celebrate the conception of Christ on the 25th of March and his birth on the 25th of December (Christmas) of every calendar year. The virgin birth of Jesus is not to be confused with the Roman Catholic doctrine known as the 'immaculate conception', which relates to Mary's own conception.

Koran: **The Virgin Birth**

Jesus is repeatedly referred to in the Koran as 'Isa bin Maryam' (Jesus, son of Mary), with mother and son held in high esteem. Maryam is the only woman named in the Koran. Furthermore, of the Korans 114 chapters she is among only eight people honoured with a chapter bearing their name. The chapter dedicated to Maryam recounts the story of her purity, her virginity, and indeed her conception and birthing of her son. Her virgin purity and moral spotlessness leading up to, and after her perfect conception (a conception without sin), elevates Maryam above all women; verses describe her as 'chosen one' (Koran 3: 42), and 'purified one' (Koran 3: 42). The Islamic view is that the angel Jibril (Gabriel) was sent by Allah to speak with Maryam and inform her that she would soon expect to bear a son. This visitation by the archangel Jibril with the message of conception was however not Maryam's first encounter with celestial angels. The above chapter in the Koran enlightens its readers that angels had visited Maryam on other occasions to notify her of her valued status among humanity. The Koran passages affirm that her son Jesus was indeed the outcome of an untainted virgin birth. Maryam's husband Joseph and the meagre setting of a manger as the birthplace of Christ do not appear in the Koran. The spiritual conception is a wonder credited more to the life of Maryam than that of Christ. Islam does not accept that the virgin birth is undeniable evidence of the godliness of Jesus. In Islam the spiritual implications of the virgin birth is equal to the creation of Adam, and in fact, some argue that the creation of Adam (the first human) is a more miraculous creation, as Adam was 'born' without father *or* mother. Maryam was a human fit for the company of angels and the touch of divinity; the only woman to make the transition from virgin to motherhood a truly unimaginable and wondrous happening.

So... what's the point of the virgin birth?

Bible: **Prophet of Nazareth**

Jesus is the supreme figure of Christianity. He founded the church, performed miracles, and rose from the dead. In modern terminology the word 'Christ' refers explicitly to Jesus of Nazareth. By and large Christians await the second coming of Jesus, when the remainder of the messianic prophesies will be fulfilled. Jesus is one of the three divine elements that make up the Holy Trinity; the Father, the Son, and the Holy Spirit. Jesus began his public ministry of teaching and miracles at 'about thirty years of age'. He spoke in proverbs and tales, banished demons, defended the oppressed, and taught about the kingdom of God. His ministry was shorted lived, lasting approximately three years. The four gospels combined are the main sources of the biography of Christ: covering his nativity, mission, death sentence, and resurrection, as a fulfilment of the prophecies found in the Old Testament. At the height of his ministry, Jesus led twelve male disciples and attracted crowds of thousands, mostly in the areas of Galilee and Perea. His sermons and long discourses focused on service and modesty, forgiveness of sin, faith, turning the other cheek, love for friends and enemies, and upholding the law. He reached out to the poor, the Samaritans, and to foreigners, and making a point of speaking to sinners, because it is the sick that need physicians, not the healthy. Jesus visited Jerusalem during the Passover festival and enjoyed the Passover feast with his disciples. His tone soon changed into a farewell speech and talk of betrayal by one of his own, which would lead to his execution. Later on in a nearby garden Jesus is ambushed by temple guards, Judas Iscariot is there to identify him to the guards with a kiss, and he is arrested. The Jewish leaders turn him over to Pilate for execution, but Pilate is reluctant to act and Pilate's wife, tormented by a dream, urges him not to take part in sentencing the prophet. Pilate renounces all responsibility and sends Jesus to Herod Antipas. Jesus is found guilty of treason and crucified. He died before late afternoon at Calvary. The Gospels tell of the darkening of the sky from twelve until three that afternoon. Jesus rose from the dead on the Sunday. After his resurrection he commands his apostles to "make disciples of all nations."

Koran: **Prophet of Nazareth**

The Koran refers to Isa (Jesus), a total of twenty five times; mostly as 'Ibn Maryam' (son of Mary), 'nabi' (prophet), 'rasul' (messenger of Allah), and 'al Masih' (anointed one). The origin of Jesus in the Koran text begins with the birth of his mother Maryam, and her life in the temple of Jerusalem. Jesus was born as the result of a miraculous virgin birth by the order of Allah and endowed with the power to perform miracles by Allah's consent, not by his own authority. None of Jesus' disciples are named in the Koran and he was accompanied by a far greater number of followers (up to 72). He was divinely chosen to preach the truth of a single God and submission to the will of God by calling all to follow the 'path of righteousness'. Like all prophets who preach the acceptance of a divine 'path' outlined by God (Sharia in Islam), Jesus was therefore Muslim (a person who submits to the will of Allah). Also, like all Allah's prophets, he was a mortal being. This in effect limits the powers of Jesus and removes any right of godliness or lineage with God; dissolving any share in divinity. Jesus in the Koran is a mortal man and anything more is rejected. To believe that Jesus was the direct son of God is to reject God's divine oneness (tawhid). Jesus himself does not declare to be the son of God in the Koran and it is written that Jesus will deny ever making such claims to divinity at the last judgement after his return. Jesus served as a precursor to the Prophet Muhammad; he announced the coming of Muhammad in the Koran and allegedly makes a similar report in the New Testament Bible. In the Gospel of John, the coming of the 'Paraclete' is foretold; this prediction is believed by some Muslims to be a reference to the Prophet Muhammad. Passages of the Koran refute the crucifixion of Jesus as expressed in the Bible. The Islamic view holds that the end of Christ occurred through his bodily ascension to heaven and not on the cross. Greater understanding of this view is linked to the significance of Judas Iscariot. The second coming of Jesus also appears in the Koran; it is foretold that he will return during the end times to defeat the antichrist (Ad-Dajjal).

Bible: **The Last Prophet of Islam**

There are no biblical prophecies or references made to the Prophet Muhammad by name, faith or spiritual following present in the Holy Bible.

Koran: **The Last Prophet of Islam**

The Arabian city of Mecca is the birthplace of the Prophet Muhammad; the last prophet of Islam and originator of the Islamic unified religion. He could neither read nor write, yet excelled as a trader, philosopher, ambassador, public speaker, law maker, military general, and reformer. However he is most noted for his position as a spiritual messenger of divine order. Orphaned at childhood, he was raised by his uncle Abu Talib in good health and married his first wife at age twenty five. He was a meditative thinker and during his forties chose to reflect in the peace and quiet of the caves of the nearby mountains, where, during the month of Ramadan, he received his first revelation from Allah through a visitation from the angel Jibril (Gabrielle). He began preaching three years later and gained a small number of followers, coupled with some open hostility from several Meccan tribes. To escape further ill-treatment he migrated to Medina in the year 622 and successfully united conflicting tribes, increased his followers to ten thousand, and ultimately defeated the Meccan tribes to occupy Mecca. In 632, after a return journey to Medina from his farewell pilgrimage, Muhammad took ill and passed away. By the time of his death, most of the Arabian Peninsula had converted to Islam. He had victoriously united the tribes into a single Muslim community. The revelations which Muhammad received until his death shape the verses of the Koran (Qur'an, Quran, Coran or Al-Quran), universally noted as the perfect book and finest piece of literature in the Arabic Language. The primary source of knowledge about Muhammad is based upon the Koran, with the exception of the hadith (sayings and practices of the Prophet Muhammad). During his lifetime Muhammad had thirteen wives, mostly to strengthen political alliances. His youngest wife Aisha was known as his favourite wife. She survived him by decades and was active in compiling the Hadith literature in Sunni tradition. Every day Muslims all over the world use the salutation which was taught by the Prophet Muhammad. 'May peace be upon you', which in Arabic is 'As-Salamu 'alaykum'. This phrase is one of the most instantly recognizable greeting gestures in the world.

The family unit is the greatest unit of measurement.

Chapter 9

The Ties That Bind

Bible: **People and Places**

Over fifty people identified in the Bible appear in the verses of the Koran. What's more, these similarities include many well known events and revelations. The Biblical accounts typically contain descriptive verses, narrative detail, and appearing in sequential order, whilst the Koran accounts are presented as parables and moral teachings, often containing very little by way of detail. Researchers, students, and avid readers of the Koran have been known to refer to the Bible in order to develop a more detailed picture of the person or event revealed in the Koran. Many of the narratives contain the same significant figures and events; from the legendary conflict of David and Goliath (Dawud and Jalut in the Koran), historic leaders such as the iconic Moses, the martyr Jesus, and the wise king Solomon; to the brothers Cain and Abel (Qabil and Abel), and the lawless cities of Sodom and Gomorrah. And during earths darkest days when the entire world was engulfed by a great flood and humanity was compelled to start over, the story of Noah's Ark, makes an appearance in the Koran (Nuh and the flood). The single most important similarity between biblical and Koran texts is that both books declare that the creation of the world was by a single almighty and all powerful God. Once a person becomes even slightly familiar with both Holy books, the overall similarity found in the timeless stories, the moving poetry, meaningful ethical teachings, and rebuking, is really quite astounding. The awe and marvel of these similarities may be considered a revelation in itself.

Not!

Yes But Corrupted

?

Not!

— copied Bible accounts

Koran: **People and Places**

The Koran approves of the association it has with earlier religious books namely, the torah and the gospel, speaking well of both sacred writings. The Koran attributes the similarities it shares with the Bible to a unique origin that both holy books share, declaring that all the books (Torah, Bible and Koran) have been revealed by the very same God, the one true God Allah. Therefore the common elements or similarities between the Koran and the Bible exist due to this common divine source. The Koran also acknowledges that the original Jewish and Christian sacred texts were authentic revelations from God (Allah) to the Jewish and Christian Prophets, however, Muslims accept as true, that those original writings have been neglected, corrupted, and altered over time. As a result of this, the holy books of the Jewish and Christian peoples have been replaced by another sacred book, a later text considered to be the final holy book to be revealed by Allah. This perfect book has remained so because it has never been re-written or altered, this book is the Holy Koran. The Koran does recount stories from the Christian Bible but differs in many details. For instance, the stories contained in the Koran concentrate on the moral or deeply spiritual significance of the tales with less emphasis on the narrative and the descriptive. There are guiding principles that outline the way Muslims are to comprehend the books of the Bible. The foremost rule is that the Koran is at all times more authoritative. Therefore, biblical accounts that support the Koran versions are accepted by Muslims. The similarities in biblical Scripture that do not support the views held by the Koran are rejected.

Bible: **And the Torah**

Torah (meaning 'instruction' or 'law' in Hebrew), is often identified as the 'Pentateuch'. The Torah is the first five parts of the Hebrew Bible (the Tanakh), which is the founding religious document of Judaism. The Holy scriptures that form the Torah are ancient and remain the collection of five sacred books: The book of Genesis, Exodus, Leviticus, Numbers and Deuteronomy. Outside of its central significance in Judaism, the Torah is accepted by Christianity as part of the Bible, comprising the first five books of the Old Testament. For that reason the typical point of view of the Holy Bible for the layman, is a collection of sacred scriptures of both Judaism and Christianity. The Christian Bible is divided into two parts: The first part called the Old Testament, containing the 39 books of Hebrew Scripture, and the second portion called the New Testament, containing a set of 27 books of which there is the Gospel and the life of Christ.

Koran: **And the Torah**

The Torah (Tawrat to Muslims), is the first five sections of the Hebrew Bible (the Tanakh), and is considered by Muslims to be the word of Allah revealed to Moses. According to Jewish tradition, the Torah was revealed to Moses at Mount Sinai and contains the commandments of God that provide the basis for Jewish religious law. Under Islam, the original Torah is well respected because Muslims believe in the prophet-hood of Moses, which is one of the fundamental faiths of Islam. However the Muslim faith accepts the original Torah only. The viewpoint within the Islamic community is that the original revelation (the earliest Torah), has been tainted and made imperfect over time, thus making the present Jewish version Torah not at all valued by Islamic nations. The Koran speaks greatly of Moses and reports the certainty of his existence and his teachings, triumphs, and religious guidelines that Allah revealed to the Children of Israel. The Holy Koran confirms the original revelations contained in the Torah and also validates the Gospel of the Christian Bible and acknowledges the connection between all three books of God. With the Koran itself, recognised as God's final word.

"He has sent down upon you, [O Muhammad], the Book in truth (the Koran), confirming what was before it. And He revealed the Taurat (the Torah) and the Injeel (the Gospel)" (Koran 3:3).

The value of enlightenment is difficult to measure. I can say with certainly however, that it is more than a little, and less than a lot.

Chapter 10

The International Game of Numbers

Bible: **The Numbers**

Religion: Christianity. Place of worship: the church, cathedral, temple, and mission. Title of local leader: priest, pastor, minister, and elder. Sacred texts: the Bible. Cultural tradition: Abrahamic religion. Major territories covered: Europe, the Americas, Oceania, Sub-Saharan Africa, the Philippines, and South Korea, including sizeable population areas in Japan, Russia, and Hong Kong. Percentage of the world population: approximately 33% (and falling). Of the 6.6 billion human inhabitants on God's green earth it is estimated that about 2.1 billion (33%) of its citizens are followers of the Christian faith. Annual growth rates within the denominations of Christianity: Pentecostal: 8.1% annual growth, Evangelicals: 5.4% annual growth, All Protestants: 3.3% annual growth, and Roman Catholics and Others amount to 1.3% annual growth. By comparison the growth rate of Roman Catholicism appears to be dipping gradually. The fall in the Christian annual growth rate is attributed to a decline in church attendance and the low Christian birth-rate. For example, in the year 2008 the Office for National Statistics in the United Kingdom revealed that the number of Christians in the country fell by more than 2 million over a 4 year period.

Koran: **The Numbers**

Religion: Islam. Place of worship: mosque (masjid). Title of local leader: imam. Sacred Texts: the Koran and the Hadith. Cultural tradition: Abrahamic religion. Percentage of the world population: approx. 21% (and rising). Major territories covered: the Middle East, Northern Africa, Central Asia, South Asia, Western Africa, and the Malay Archipelago; including sizeable population areas in Eastern Africa, the Balkan Peninsula and China. It is approximated that of the 6.6 billion human occupants on the planet earth, about 1.5 billion (21%) of the earths residents are followers of the Islamic faith (Shi'a, Sunni, Sufi, et cetera). Of the largest world religions, Islam is the fastest growing faith with an estimated annual growth rate of about 2.7%. Many official census and survey groups assign the rapidly increasing figures of the annual Muslim growth rate to that of the Muslim birth rate which is generally greater than the Christian birth rate. This coupled with the rate of conversions to Islam and recorded immigration patterns. For example, in the year 2008 the Office for National Statistics in the United Kingdom revealed that the increasing Muslim population in Britain had grown by 'more than 500,000 to 2.4 million in just four years'. The population multiplied 10 times faster than the rest of British society.

Bible: **The League of Nations**

Top 10 nations with the highest percentage of Christians

UN Ranking	Country	Christian (2002/2010)
Rank [1]	Vatican City:	100%
Rank [2]	Pitcairn Islands:	100%
Rank [3]	Ecuador:	99.0%
Rank [4]	East Timor:	99.0%
Rank [5]	Armenia:	98.7%
Rank [6]	Equatorial Guinea:	98.6%
Rank [7]	Moldova:	98.3%
Rank [8]	U.S. Samoa:	98.3%
Rank [9]	Venezuela:	98.0%
Rank [10]	Greece:	98.0%

The top seven nations with the largest population of Christians

Ranking	Country	Christians (2010)
Rank [1]	United States of America:	243,186,000
Rank [2]	Brazil:	174,700,000
Rank [3]	Mexico:	105,095,000
Rank [4]	Russia:	99,775,000
Rank [5]	Philippines:	90,530,000
Rank [6]	Nigeria:	76,281,000
Rank [7]	China: Peoples Republic:	66,959,000

(See page 143 for resource materials)

Koran: **The League of Nations**

Top 10 countries with the highest percentage of Muslims

Ranking (2009)	Country	Muslims	Percentage
Rank [1]	Afghanistan:	28,072,000	99.7%
Rank [2]	Tunisia:	10,216,000	99.5%
Rank [3]	Iran:	73,333,000	99.4%
Rank [4]	Western Sahara:	510,000	99.4%
Rank [5]	Azerbaijan:	8,765,000	99.2%
Rank [6]	Yemen:	23,363,000	99.1%
Rank [7]	Mauritania:	3,261,000	99.1%
Rank [8]	Niger:	15,075,000	98.6%
Rank [9]	Somalia:	8,995,000	98.5%
Rank [10]	Maldives:	304,000	98.4%

The top seven nations with the largest population of Muslims

Rank	Country	Muslims (2009)
Rank [1]	Indonesia	202,867,000
Rank [2]	Pakistan	174,082,000
Rank [3]	India	160,945,000
Rank [4]	Bangladesh	145,312,000
Rank [5]	Egypt	78,513,000
Rank [6]	Nigeria	78,056,000
Rank [7]	Iran	73,777,000

(See page 143 for resource materials)

After the darkness, comes light.

Chapter 11

The End of Earth and Everything

Bible: **The End of Earth and Everything**

The final and only book of the Bible noted for its apocalyptic content, predictions of future events, and reports of prophetic happenings, is the book of Revelation. Its passages merge (or collide) the kingdom of Heaven, and of Hell, with our world in the final battle between good and evil. The sweeping themes are of judgement, salvation, and the return of the Messiah. The cryptic narrative of 'Revelation' makes it a great source for debate among academics that endeavour to interpret its message. The End Times may refer to the end of a period in time, or an end to the age-old bond we have with God, or indeed a literal prediction of the future. The writings are part of the three main Abrahamic religions (Judaism, Christianity, and Islam), and appear in many other faiths as well, under the well known 'doomsday' scenarios. Popular art and literature interpretations refer to this great event as the 'End of Days'. In Christianity, the end times often portray a period of great tribulation on earth during the time where those left behind (after the rapture) will begin to suffer hardships, indiscriminate natural disasters, famine, distress, and wars on an extraordinary scale. Following this period will be the second coming of Christ (the Lamb of God), who will usher in the fullness of the kingdom of God, and bring an end to the suffering and evil. After the age of peace, there is a second brief period of difficulty which results in the everlasting removal of the wicked. After which a new heaven and a new earth will replace the old realms and the people of God will journey to the presence of God, and of Christ, in a new heavenly city. Revelation identifies the Beast allied with the number 666; the false prophet, the great harlot Babylon, and the four horsemen of the apocalypse (invasion, warfare, famine, and death), with Satan branded the 'great dragon'. Ultimately the dragon, the beast, and the false prophet, are thrown into a lake of fire. Catholicism mainly adheres to the non-literal realization of this forecast; 'Of that day and hour no one knows, not even the angels of heaven...but the Father only'. Tradition holds that these events will come to us like a 'thief in the night' (1 Thessalonians 5: 2).

Koran: **The End of Earth and Everything**

The Koran and Sunnah provide as many as one hundred signs that signal the approach of judgement day. These signs are divided into two groups; the minor signs and the major signs. There are over sixty minor signs which include: the widespread consumption of intoxicants, many women of childbearing age that will be unable to give birth, leaders of nations will become their oppressors, men will begin to resemble women and women will begin to resemble men; adultery and fornication will be carried out in public, and smog will appear over cities because of the evil committed. The above minor signs are few among many. The major signs are less in number and cover events of greater impact. Events such as the coming of the beast, and the antichrist (Masih ad-Dajjal), the sun rising from the west rather than the east, earth-shattering earthquakes that will change geographical terrain, the appearance of Isa al-Masih (Jesus Christ), and the appearance of Imam Mahdi (the final Muslim Caliph, who will aid in the destruction of evil). Islamic tradition teaches about the immortality of the human soul and traditions hold that Prophet Muhammad will be the first to be revived as the day of judgement begins. The righteous will be rewarded in Heaven and the unrighteous punished in Hell. God will hold every Muslim and non-Muslim answerable for their deeds. This event will take place on a predetermined time unknown to mankind. The final judgement of humanity involves a great apocalypse and the 'end times' literature in the Koran describes the Armageddon as 'fitna' (a test) or 'Malahim (in the shi'ite tradition). The Islamic view supports the belief that Isa (Jesus), will physically return at the time appointed by Allah, and will bring about the destruction of the antichrist. In Shia Islam there is an earthly reality that will occur before the end of human life on earth. The coming of Christ will coincide with the return of Imam Mahdi. Christ and Mahdi will join forces to bring about peace and justice on earth between all people of faith. After which Imam Mahdi will re-establish the true Islam and the world will find peace. There will be an age of rule by Imam Mahdi, and the resurrection of men and women will commence as the day of judgement begins.

Never forget a good deed, and for goodness sake,
never judge a book by its movie

davidalalade.com

holybible-holykoran.com

holybible-holyquran.com

holyquran-holybible.com

thetwinbooks.com

Face book: David Alalade

You Tube: Holy Bible Holy Koran /Book Soundtracks

Listen to the music soundtracks commissioned for the book.

Read the review by the 'U.S. Review of Books'.

With comments & emails from a global readership of fans.

Video reviews from online bloggers, writers, and fans.

A behind the scenes look at upcoming book fairs & events.

And regular updated content on the upcoming sequel:

'Holy Bible Holy Koran 2'

Coming Soon

Holy Bible Holy Koran 2
The Enemy of My Enemy is My Self

Preview of Contents

Holy Bible Holy Koran II (tentative chapter titles)

The Ten Commandments / The Significance of Lady Magdalene / The Significance of Mary the Immaculate / The Significance of Marriage / The Family / The Male Body / The Female Body / Love / Dress Code / The Garden Eden / Repentance / Suicide / Incest / Rape / Wrath / Envy / Pride / Prostitution / Gambling / Violence / Honour Killings / Revenge / Hatred / The Paedophile / Body Enhancements and the Tattoo / Peace and Mercy / War / Abortion / Contraception / The Infertile Man / The Barren Woman / The Kingdom of Hell / The Kingdom of Heaven / Angels / Demons / Lucifer: the fallen King / Human Life Span / Death / Immortality / The Creation of Artificial Life…etc

Bible: **Resource Material**

- The Holy Bible: Revised Standard Version. Holman Pub. C1982.
  Eastern Customs in Bible Lands: Hodder & Stoughton, 1894.
  The last Prophets: Anne De Graaf 1959, Bible Society. 1991.
- The Revised English Bible: Oxford University Press, 1989.
- New Testament, Psalms/Proverbs: Hodder & Stoughton, 1995
  Dictionary of proper names & places in the Bible: Odlelain and R. Seguineau, 1982.
- The Old Testament: translated out of the original tongues. Oxford University Press, 1992
  The Holy Bible:
- New International Version (©1984)
- New Living Translation (©2007)
- English Standard Version (©2001)
- New American Standard Bible (©1995)
- International Standard Version (©2008)
- King James Bible / American King James Version / American Standard Version
- Bible in Basic English / English Revised Version / Webster's Bible Translation
  World English Bible
  <u>Online Sources</u>:
  OpenBible.info
  Bible.cc
  Religious population estimates: Adherents.com

9 x BIBLES
plus the O.T. + the N.T.

Koran: **Resource Material**

The Lane Lexicon: Edward William Lane. 1998

Man in Quran and the meaning of Furqan: Surat ul Baqarah/tafsir. Fadhlalla Haeri Blanco: Zehra, c 1982

The message of the Quran: Translated and explained: Muhammad Asad. Gibralter: Dar al-Andalus; London; Distributors, Brill, 1980.

● The Koran, a new translation and presentation: Henri Mercier: Trans by L. Tremlett. London: Luzac, 1956.1975

Approaching the Quran: the early revelations: Michael Sells. Ashland Or. White Cloud Press, 1999/2001.

The Quran and the West: Kenneth Cragg. Washington D.C.: Georgetown University Press; Malisende, 2006

Islam for the Western mind: understanding Muhammad and the Koran: Richard Henry Drummond.: Hampton Roads publishing company. C2005

The Quranic precept: text, translation and commentary: Arabic text, Roman transliteration and English translation. Southampton: Sharib, 2003

Wisdom of the Koran: C. Merton Babcock and Boyd Hanna. Peter Pauper Press (1966).

Online Sources:

studyquran.co.uk

Religious population estimates: Adherents.com

1 x Qur'an.

Bible: **Till We Meet Again**

'In the name of the Father and of the Son and of the Holy Spirit'

Koran: **Till We Meet Again**

'*Bismillah al-Rahman al-Rahim*'

(In the name of God, most Gracious, most Compassionate)

CPSIA information can be obtained
at www.ICGtesting.com
Printed in the USA
LVHW041130050820
662441LV00006B/1643